The
Wedding Workout

Tracy

To my mother, Eleanor, for being the best mom she can be
and for believing in me. When you said, "Tracy, I know you can
write this book," it truly made all the difference.
I love you, Mom!

Suzanne

To Shawn, who, without your endless support, encouragement,
humor, and love, none of this would have been possible.

The Wedding Workout

Tracy Effinger
and
Suzanne Rowen

Contemporary Books

Chicago   New York   San Francisco   Lisbon   London   Madrid   Mexico City
Milan   New Delhi   San Juan   Seoul   Singapore   Sydney   Toronto

Library of Congress Cataloging-in-Publication Data

Effinger, Tracy.
   The wedding workout : look and feel fabulous on your special day / Tracy Effinger and Suzanne Rowen.
     p. cm.
   Includes index.
   ISBN 0-07-138916-4
    1. Exercise for women. 2. Brides—Health and hygiene. I. Rowen, Suzanne. II. Title.

RA778.E336 2002
646.7'042—dc21   2001052164

Contemporary Books

A Division of The **McGraw·Hill** *Companies*

ISBN 0-07-138916-4

This book was set in Vendetta by Laurie Young
Illustrations by Elisa Cohen
Cover and interior photographs by Albane Navizet
Cover design by Tom Lau
Creative concept by Tracy Effinger

Printed and bound by Quebecor World/Hawkins

Contents

Acknowledgments

A special thanks from Tracy to my family: Mom, Dad, Millar, and Laura Effinger, to Guru Singh, Espn Tompter, all of my students who show up over and over again for class, Sela Ward, Paula Wagner, Amy Brenneman, Will and Viv, Marki Costello, Erroll Dorschell, Jon Congdon, Heather Faye, and Tricia Munford. John Bouton, Michale Monteroso. Thank you all for supporting, loving, and inspiring me in all of your various ways through the writing process.

A special thanks from Suzanne to Shirley and David Rowen, Elizabeth Marks, Tammy Fine, David Markman, Blaine and Jeane of Rainbow Photography, Valerie, Norma and Eduardo of Celeste Bridal Salon, and my running buddies, Melissa, Michael, and Louise.

Finally, we would like to thank our editor, Nancy Hancock, our publicist, Lisa Elia, our photographer, Albane Navizet, Robyn DeBell for her nutrition expertise , Rena Copperman, Laurie Young, Elisa Cohen, Sara Chameides for hair and make-up, and our agent, Michael Broussard.

Introduction

So, you're engaged. You're so excited you can't contain yourself. You want to tell the UPS man and the guy behind the counter at the cleaners. You feel like you're the only woman in the world getting married. Well-wishers abound with cries of "congratulations" and "when is the big day?" The spotlight is on you. It can be exciting and overwhelming at the same time. We hope this book will help to ease your mind and provide some answers for you, as well as get you into fantastic shape, during this whirlwind time before your big day.

Suzanne

I know that almost every altar-bound woman, whether fit or flabby, has concerns about her body as the big day approaches, and I am no exception. Getting married makes you take a good look at yourself. My fiancé, who already thought I looked great, said I was insane to be concerned about my appearance.

Let's face it, I doubt there are any women out there who roll out of bed on their wedding day without a care in the world, put on a burlap sack, and head toward the chapel with bed head. This is your big day, your Hollywood premiere, and all eyes will be on you. It is natural to feel some anxiety about the way you look. At this point, we know you've won your fiancé over. He's asked you to marry him. That doesn't change the fact that you want to feel fantastic when you exchange your vows.

Regardless of your age, you may feel the need for a "body makeover." The body you had at twenty-one may have exited the building, or maybe you are just a little low-energy these days and need to get back on track. I already had a relatively healthy diet and exercise regime but after scrutinizing myself in various wedding dresses, I knew I needed a new approach. I began to watch my nutrition more closely. I increased my activity with more running, yoga, weight training, and a weekly tennis match.

A few months into our engagement, however, I became frustrated with the lack of results in relation to my efforts. This frustration led to the idea for this book. I figured there were tons of normal women out there like myself, trying to juggle work and everyday stresses while planning a wedding and attempting to stay healthy.

Tracy

One night after class, Suzanne came to me with the idea for the Wedding Workout. She was feeling discouraged about her body and needed some help getting ready for her big day. It made me think about how, in all of my years of training people, I have worked with brides, grooms, bridesmaids, groomsmen, and more brides. In fact, I devoted a whole year to one client who was a bridesmaid three times in one year (we called her training "Bridesmaid 2000"). Getting married is a prime motivator to get in shape, yet as a bride-to-be it is easy to let fitness fall by the wayside. While many of my clients are successful actresses or actors and all of them are busy individuals, a bride-to-be is more than a full-time job. You've got your dress, the food, the showers, the parties, the out-of-towners, the gifts, the flowers, your hair, his hair, and, most importantly, your dress and how you look and feel on your big day. I'm here to tell you it is time to make your health a priority. Establish it now as a must in your life, and you will bring energy, confidence, and vitality into your marriage. What could be more important than that?

Like any good teachers, we want to see you create a strong and positive self-image, along with a new physique. We want you to go down that aisle with your head held high, your shoulders back, and a kick in your step. This is not always an easy process, but we are here to help! It's scary to take on a new challenge—think how we felt when we had to start writing this book. It seemed like an impossible and overwhelming task, but simply committing to it was the first and hardest step. After getting the ball rolling, things started falling into place.

We know that the same will be true for you as you get started here. When you commit to following the workout plan provided in this book, and you use this book as your own personal guide, you can consider us your own personal trainer and support system.

While you are undertaking the Wedding Workout, keep this book with you at all times. Consider it a permanent part of your purse along with your wedding planner, hairbrush, lipstick, wallet, cell phone, and PDA. Every day be diligent in your reading and writing, it will help you stay honest, focused, and on track. You are going to be the belle of the ball, and by following the Wedding Workout you can bet you are going to be the bomb.

With that said, let's get in shape!

Where You Are Now

First, let's take a good look at where you are today. It is important to love and accept your body as it is, flaws and all, because it has brought you this far. Wherever you are is okay. He loves you! You've got a ring on your finger and a twinkle in your eye. Look at *The Wedding Workout* as your personal tool for fine-tuning: the fillet instead of a burger, the pie instead of just the apple. Do not beat yourself up about your body. Think of this as a starting point. The you that will walk down the aisle is the same you now, only we're going to sharpen your edges, access your energy, and create a bride who will surely glow. You're going to shed what you don't need, clean the closets (so to speak), and prepare your mind and body for your future.

First, let's check in on self-image. Are you a positive thinker or a negative thinker? What role does fitness play in your life? In your fiancé's? What is your ideal body? How do you see yourself looking and feeling on your wedding day? What is your fantasy wedding dress? Can you imagine a workout class with your bridesmaids or a nice run on the morning of your big day? What would you like to learn about or experience with your body? What positive changes in yourself do you want to make? Do you want to feel sexier? Do you wear thongs? Garters? Would you like to? Would you dare to?? Do you believe you can have the body you want? Want to try? If you follow the Wedding Workout we can get you going and keep you going toward that dream.

Now, let's talk about commitment. You have to commit to the Wedding Workout in the same way that you commit to planning your wedding. That means scheduling your training sessions, meals, and snacks exactly the same way you would schedule appointments with your wedding coordinator, photographer, dressmaker, and cake maker. Commit now and it won't be a last-minute "Oh, my God, I'm never going to look the way that I want to on my wedding day," nor will it be a quick fix based on not eating and fad-diet gimmicks. Your priorities of looking great and feeling fabulous will help you create new habits, as well as a new you. We challenge you to engage in a more fit life, for better or for worse, in hopefully less sickness and more health, from now until death do you part.

Now, let's begin to look at some ways to think about your goals and provide some benchmarks in order to chart your progress. Not to put a damper on such a happy time, but this means we are going to have to take your weight and measurements, as well as assess your food habits and exercise regimen. The idea here is not to focus on numbers or make you feel bad, but to help you learn more about yourself. Also, by assessing your weight and measurements on your own first, you won't have any surprises at the bridal shop. Hopefully, the margin for discomfort and self-consciousness will diminish! Remember, you can change your body! Just think how empowering it will be the closer you get to your wedding day to look back at where you started.

Taking measurements and weighing yourself may very well be the hardest part of the Wedding Workout. After all, no woman we know, regardless of her size, really likes to weigh or measure herself. However, the joy and elation a woman experiences the first time she sees the scale go down and the measurements decrease make the initial pain of weighing and measuring all worthwhile. By charting your progress, you can be assured you have some control. The slightest decrease builds confidence and supercharges the drive to continue. On those days when you're "feeling fat," you can do a reality check and assess if it is just in your head or if you need to refocus and get back on track.

Still, weighing and measuring can be a very emotional and scary process for us all. Although they are just numbers, they carry a lot of emotional weight. Many of our feelings about these numbers developed in our childhood and teen years. Just stepping on a scale can trigger very uncomfortable and painful feelings of inadequacy and fear. We have included a journal page on page 4 for you to use to express some of these feelings. Write about your scale rage and phobias with fervor! Go for it! Get it out! Remember the scale is just a scale. It is an inhuman, dumb object that has no say about who you are or how valuable you are as a person and as a bride! It is just a scale. Don't allow it to weigh you down!

MAINTAINING YOUR BODY INNOCENCE

At birth, we are all born with a body. We spend the first ten years or so just being in our bodies until we learn somewhere along the way that our body is not okay. Can you remember when as a little girl you had no understanding of weight or body image? This is what we refer to as *body innocence*. You did not yet know that

Getting on the scale makes me feel . . .

there could be anything wrong with your body or that you should be a certain weight. In other words, it wasn't something that bothered you until someone or something taught you it should.

Tracy

In fifth-grade PE class, I remember getting on the scale in front of everyone and seeing the arrow hit the 100-pound mark. One girl exclaimed, "Wow! That's a lot!" Like her, I, too, was shocked, because at ten years old I truly didn't understand how my body could weigh 100 pounds. I was one of the taller girls in my class and I felt elephantine, gargantuan, like the *Titanic*. I was so sad that I was not the little, cute one, and I felt unlovable and not special. Unfortunately, these are feelings about my body size that still come up in me today.

Try to remember when you first learned your body was not okay. When did you first learn the concept of dieting? When did weight, numbers, and sizes start to have so much power in your life? It seems we have all been told we are too tall, too short, too skinny, too fat, too big, too flat, too something! At some point, outside influences taught us that there are such things as diets, that you can't always eat what you want, that you must be perfect to be healthy, etc. Somewhere along the way we bought into the idea that we are what we weigh! By facing our numbers, hopefully we can acknowledge that we don't have to be victims of them.

Regardless of what you have been told about your body, your body can change its shape by a large degree through diet and exercise. Get excited!!! We can do a lot before the big day! Try to recover the freedom of thought of a little girl who has not yet been influenced by the world's opinion about how she should look. That little girl is still living within you. She's the one who wants to play when you have a big project due for work, the one who flirted shamelessly with your now-fiancé when you first met, and she is sometimes the one who coaxes you into eating that pint of ice cream when you're desperately trying to watch your diet. Don't forget that the little girl inside of you is going to walk down the aisle, too, so let's concentrate on providing a nurturing and loving place for her to grow into a fit and happy bride.

WEIGHING IN

You will need a scale, a tape measure, and a pen. If you would like to take a "before" photo, you can. If you have written your journal entry regarding the scale and you still don't feel ready to get on, don't. Don't worry about it! Perhaps the scale is just not for you! If you are willing to get on, know that some negative feelings may come up and be prepared to deal with them. Be ready to write about your feelings, cry if you need to, or call a friend and figure out something really nice you can do for yourself.

You may find that repeatedly getting on the scale also helps to diminish the scary scale syndrome. Like pulling a stuck car out of the mud, you can reverse your negative thoughts and focus on the positive, exciting process ahead of you. You have a plan of action and you are making positive choices. This is your time! So before stepping on, be prepared for the attack of your negative, self-critical thoughts. The negative thoughts will appear as though they are the absolute truth

Tracy

I know that for me, the hardest part of getting on a scale is the fact that there is absolutely nothing I can do in that moment to change the number. I am stuck! I am where I am, and I can't be anywhere else. There is no immediate fix, and almost always I feel an overwhelming sense of helplessness, doom, and despair. As the number reveals itself, I often become consumed with feelings of shame, self-hate, and inadequacy. I get scared about the process of having to change and not being sure if I can do it. But by standing tall in the face of these feelings and knowing that you have the power to change, I promise you they won't last long and will lose their power.

over which you have no power—but you do! Think about what your body can do, not how much it weighs. Take a deep, loving breath of acceptance, knowing that you are a capable, powerful woman. Now step on that scale, stand tall, look down at that number, and repeat after me, "Nah-nah-nah-nah-nah-nah—I have a plan." Congratulations! Trust that you are stepping into the most powerful you that you can possibly be, even if you can't see her yet! She is there! And you're heading not only to the altar but also to a stronger, happier, sexier, hotter, more delicious, and more yummy you!

Finally, you must also remember that body weight is not always the best indicator of what your body looks like. Your weight only tells you how much you weigh. It does not describe your body composition. It does not tell you how many pounds of you are fat as opposed to lean muscle mass. Lean muscle mass weighs more than fat, so as you burn fat and gain muscle with the Wedding Workout, remember you may lose inches without losing tons of weight. Therefore, be sure to monitor your measurements as well as weighing in. Do not be disappointed if the number on the scale is not dropping drastically. You will look and feel better regardless of any of "the numbers"! As you tone up and lose fat, your measurements will decrease, and they are the best indicator of your progress.

TAKING YOUR MEASUREMENTS

Since you are getting married and you will be picking out a dress, there is really no way to avoid taking your measurements. Remember, all the preparatory rules for getting on the scale apply here. Again, we have provided a journal page (see page 9) to help you unleash and release any judgmental thoughts and painful feelings you have. Following the journal page, we encourage you to write a love letter (see page 10) to each and every body part, thanking it for what it does for you. Think about how amazing your body truly is! Although it may not look exactly the way you would like, it is pretty darn miraculous. Just as with the scale, you don't have to be a victim of a measuring tape, either. Forget all the Playboy bunny stereotypical measurements that you have always hated comparing yourself to. Scream out loud if you have to: "No! I am not a Playboy bunny!" Feel better now? How many women do you actually know who can naturally claim to be 36-24-36? Not too many. If you happen to be a Playboy bunny, consider yourself blessed and celebrate that, too!

You may decide to enlist the help of a supportive friend to take your measurements. In preparation for the Wedding Workout, we are going to take your

Get out your negative thoughts about your body here! Uncensored!
If you don't feel negative about a body part, hooray!
Skip it. You're halfway there. Leave those negative thoughts behind.

Hair: _____

Eyes: _____

Nose: _____

Cheeks: _____

Lips: _____

Ears: _____

Freckles, moles,
    and birthmarks: _____

Neck: _____

Shoulders: _____

Breasts: _____

Hips: _____

Stomach: _____

Arms: _____

Hands: _____

Derriere: _____

Thighs and legs: _____

Feet and toes: _____

Love Letter to My Body

measurements in seven places: your neck, shoulders, upper arms, chest, waist, hips, and thighs. Include any others you would like. Now, now . . . be a good bride-to-be and don't suck in or pull the tape too tight. Measure to the nearest quarter inch and record your numbers in the chart on page 12. Get excited!!! You are at the starting line and you are about to take off! Every six weeks you are literally going to measure the progress you are making! You can change your body. Taking a good look at where you are now will help you release fear, build confidence, trust yourself, and get stronger!

TAKING EMOTIONAL STOCK

We have all at one time or another wished for some part of our body to be miraculously revamped overnight. The thing to remember is that it is the parts that make us different and uniquely beautiful.

It is now time to take emotional stock before you embark on your Wedding Workout journey. Everyone knows that getting married, though exciting, can be an overwhelming experience and also an emotional one. Whether you're tying the knot at twenty-one or sixty-five, there is a part of yourself that you're leaving behind as you begin your new life with the one you love.

This brings us to your emotional trousseau. A trousseau is defined as the possessions, such as clothes or linens, that a bride prepares to take with her for her marriage. This definition harkens back to days of yore. The modern definition refers to the bride-to-be's assembling her shower outfits, rehearsal dinner attire, and honeymoon apparel, such as bathing suits or sexy lingerie, before her wedding day. For this exercise, however, we'd like you to think in terms of an emotional trousseau rather than a material one. (See page 13.)

Pre-Bridal Bod
Chest: _____
Hips: _____
Neck: _____
Shoulders: _____
Thighs: _____
Upper arms: _____
Waist: _____

So the question is: What things will you pack in your emotional trousseau to take with you and what will you leave behind? It is easy to cling to ideas and behavior patterns that are familiar. But these things are heavy baggage and a change of attitude might lighten your load. That's not to say that some of your old ways may not benefit you in your new stage of life, but emotionally, how do you want to feel when you take your vows beside your husband? Do you want to feel sexy, energetic, and confident? Of course you do.

Make a list of the positive attributes
you want to pack in your trousseau.

The reality is, your state of prewedding fitness may be weighing you down or making you apprehensive about your new life. Don't let negative feelings undermine your best efforts to stay on your fitness plan.

> ## Suzanne
>
> I was scared that I wouldn't have enough time to reach my fitness goals or that I wouldn't reach them at all. I decided that I needed to start packing my emotional trousseau. I said good-bye to my old body and negative habits. The first thing that went into my trousseau was a positive attitude. I knew that with the right outlook and a little patience with myself, I could accomplish anything. To go along with my new mind-set, I packed a little willpower to help me get through the ice-cream aisle at the market. Then I tossed in confidence to help me reach my goals, big and small. Finally, I made room in my trousseau for pride—pride in who I am, sexy at any size or shape. ॰

We encourage you to leave all negative thoughts behind. You know, the ones that whisper, "You can't do it," or "You slipped off your eating plan and all is lost." In fact, make it a habit to avoid negative self-talk, or what we call "body bashing," altogether. You are your words and your perceptions. If they are negative, you will feel negative and act on that negativity. Know that there will be difficult days. So, you broke down and ate that colossal chocolate-chip cookie at the office party. Beating yourself up about it is only wasting energy. Tomorrow is another day.

Be good to yourself and set realistic goals, goals that you can reach amidst all the prewedding craziness. A realistic goal is to become a fitter, healthier *you* for your wedding day, not to expect to look like Claudia Schiffer and then be disappointed when you don't. Besides, he's marrying *you*! He loves *you*!! Visualize how you want to look and feel on your wedding day, your honeymoon, and every day thereafter, and then *go for it*.

2

What's the "Right" Size, Anyway?

Congratulations! You completed the weigh-and-measure chapter of *The Wedding Workout*. Your willingness to come this far should make you proud. You have decided to undergo a process that many people fear and avoid. You have committed to going deeper within yourself. What did you learn about your body from the previous chapter? What parts would you like to work on? What parts do you really like? What are your goals for the next few months? Are they realistic? What size do you want to be? Are you there now and would just like to firm up, or would you like to lose 5, 10, 15, or more pounds? Can you determine what the right size is for you despite all the media images out there and societal pressures to be thin? What would really make you happy?

Along with your decision to be healthier, we encourage you to look beyond what appears to be true in magazines and on TV and decide for yourself what size you would really like to be. What feels natural, normal, and comfortable to you? Remember, you and your body truly are unique, and you must embrace that as a positive and real part of who you are. Women come in a multitude of shapes and sizes. A woman who is a size 14 may be fit or unfit; same with a woman who is a size 4. A woman who is a size 10, perhaps, is simply meant to be a size 10. Telling a woman who is a size 12 to be a size 6 may be as unrealistic and harmful as telling a woman who is a size 4 that she should be a size 8. In other words, we appreciate that there are redwood trees as well as maple trees in the world, and sometimes things are fine just the way they are.

Have you ever gone clothes shopping and been able to fit into a size 6 skirt but not into a size 10 pair of jeans? How discouraging is that? Especially since the momentary feeling of size 6 victory is annihilated as soon as you try on a size 10 that barely fits! The truth is that size is relative and really depends on what we call the two Ms: measurements and manufacturer.

Everyone has unique measurements. Some people have to take the next size up just because they have a long torso or a full-size booty. A size label in a garment means almost nothing and yet it is one more number that we allow to torture us. A size 8 sewn into a garment does not tell your measurements nor does it tell you how much muscle you have or what a beautiful body you have. For most women we know, it just seems to reinforce what you're not. Here's an interesting fact. If we were shopping in the 1970s for some trippy bellbottoms, a size 12 would be about the same as a current size 12. But in the 1940s, a current size 12 would have been labeled a much smaller size, probably a 2 or 4! Ugh! As you can tell, size labels are simply symbols, and frustrating ones at that.

The other size variable is manufacturer. The manufacturers and designers decide what the showroom model size will be. The patterns are based on specific people that they want to use as models. So, Calvin Klein uses one model for his size 6 while Donna Karan uses a different model with different measurements to determine the same size. Wait, it gets even more confusing. The equivalent Japanese size 6 will be completely different due to the proportions of a typical Japanese woman. Japanese people are generally petite and small boned. The bottom line is that there are models used for patterns who we pretend represent everyone's bodies, and that is just not possible! Again, don't buy into a number to tell you who you are. Find clothes that make you feel fabulous—who cares what the size is? Don't give your power away to a number.

With *The Wedding Workout*, focus on the actions you are taking to be healthy, not just to achieve a certain body. Strive for health, and your appearance will improve naturally. No matter what your body size, being fit is always in. Being fit is never a fad. When is it cool to be out of shape? Again, if we focus on size too much, the goal can become image rather than good health. And remember, Cinderella, you have found your prince. If the glass slipper fits, wear it! As you determine your body type and size, breathe, laugh, and give yourself permission to be ordinary. In allowing yourself to be ordinary, you will most definitely find your most special and unique self. When you are not focused on getting down to a size 2 or falling victim to the latest fad, you will have a lot more fun getting healthy and getting married.

DETERMINING YOUR BODY TYPE

We are not all carbon copies of each other, but there do seem to be some general body types that consistently find their way into the female gene pool. We like to think that body types can be compared to cuts of diamonds. To help you recognize your own body type, we have created the Diamond Girls. (See pages 21–22.) Introducing Pear, Heart, Emerald, and Princess, every girl's best friends. They are sassy, sparkly, and proud of their individual cut and carat size. No matter what your size or shape, you are always a diamond—precious and unique. (And don't you forget it!) Are you a Pear cut? She's small on top with more to love on the bottom. Or are you a Heart cut? She's got it going on upstairs with less body mass down below. Maybe you're an Emerald cut. She's straight up and down, thin, and to the point. How about a Princess cut? She's petite and slightly square, with muscle to boot. Regardless of your cut, remember you are a diamond. Find your body type and let's go shopping!

Suzanne

I finally came to accept that I am a Pear-cut Diamond Girl. Once I accepted my body type, it was easier to find a dress that really flattered my figure. I needed one that would bring focus to my upper body, so I chose a gown that featured a low-cut neckline with a simple beaded design to draw attention to my chest. The elegant A-line style gives the illusion that I have a perfect hourglass shape. Look out Marilyn!

Pear

Athletic • Hourglass shape • Muscular
• More lower body mass

Heart

Generally chesty • Small hips • Thin waist
• Less lower body mass

Emerald

Small framed • Thin • Tall • Flat chest
• Lightly muscled

Princess

Short • Square and rugged
• Petite • Athletic

THE DRESS SEARCH BEGINS

Now, with your ring on your finger and a Diamond Girl "by your side," you're ready to start your dress search. Almost every woman has an idea of her perfect wedding dress. Some women have dreamt about it since childhood or have fallen in love with a dress in the pages of a bridal magazine. (Draw your fantasy dress or place a picture from a magazine of a gown you love on page 26.)

Suzanne

Reading bridal magazines is something that most brides-to-be enjoy. We can't resist it and unabashedly buy the first magazine about 20 minutes after being proposed to. I actually held out for a few days, but when I succumbed, boy did I succumb. I made the newsstand guy's day. I ran home to look at all the dresses in hopes of finding one that sparked my fancy. Model after model peered out at me from the pages. None of these women looked like me and I noticed that the air began to leak out of my balloon. I had to remind myself that in reality these women are models, not your everyday bride, and that the photographs often have been stretched, shrunk, or retouched to fool us into thinking that these women are perfect. It is also important to remember that the dresses pictured in the magazines are made in all sizes. So, if self-defeating thoughts arise in you as you peruse the pages of these bridal publications, remember these magazines should be about excitement and fun. ๛

Your dress will be your personal statement about yourself on your wedding day. The way you feel in your dress and about yourself that day will be captured in your wedding photos forever. So, take your time with dress shopping. If you need to try on twenty-five dresses, that's okay. Suzanne tried on forty-five gowns and ended up with the very first one she tried on. How's that for being completely sure? The first thing to realize, however, is that your fantasy gown may not turn out to be the right style for your body type. Don't worry, you will find a dress you love that is picture-perfect for you. Be willing to let go and keep searching! Even if you think that a strapless gown is not for you, try one on. You may be pleasantly surprised by the way it flatters your figure. To help you get a better understanding of which dresses will best suit your Diamond Girl figure, we've included the following pictures and descriptions of different dress styles. (See pages 27–33.)

Once you've had a chance to get familiar with the different bridal gowns, try your hand at our little game. Match the body type with the dress style that best suits it. (See page 34.)

Check out the following tips that will be sure to help any Diamond Girl find a gown that is flattering and fabulous. If you're tall, like Emerald, and want to deemphasize your height, a drop waist or a sheath gown will complement your figure. If you are not only tall but slender, try a ball gown, which will really highlight your silhouette. Another great trick for slender brides is to pick a gown with a heavier fabric, which will undoubtedly add weight to your look. Don't choose a gown that hides your neckline because it will only accentuate your height. Also, stay away from wacky headpieces and overly theatrical veiling.

If you want to look taller and more slender, try a dress with a higher neckline or an empire waist. Stay away from sheaths and drop waists, as they tend to create a boxier look. A short-sleeve or sleeveless dress with the right long gloves adds length to your body. Scooped necks can be very flattering. Stay away from puffy fabrics and ruffles.

If you're petite, like Princess, keep it simple. Go for a sheath or an A-line. You don't want to choose a gown that breaks your body into two parts. Stay away from big ball-gown-type dresses that will make your fiancé say, "Can I get some bride with that dress?" If you're not only petite but boxy, choose an empire or a drop waist because these styles will elongate your torso and mask your real waistline.

If you are like Pear, and want to deemphasize your bottom half and focus on your better half, choose a ball gown or an A-line dress. Make sure that the focus is on your upper body by choosing a gown with beading around the neckline. A strapless or off-the-shoulder neckline is also preferred. Steer clear of the sheath section.

If you want to deemphasize your bust and upper body, then you can relate with our Heart-cut girl. Choose a V neck or a scooped neck. Put the emphasis on your shoulders by wearing a halter neckline. If you're a Heart-cut girl who wants to emphasize her gifts, accentuate what you've got by wearing a sexy bustier or an off-the-shoulder gown. Just remember, the focus should be on your smiling face, your most important asset. For all you other Diamond Girls who want to endow your upper body, follow Heart's lead and get a great bustier that actually boosts.

Draw your fantasy dress or place a picture from a magazine of a gown you love.

Basque Waist

Full Skirt with Fitted Bodice that Comes to a "V" Below the Waist

☑ Full figures, Heart cut, Emerald cut

☒ Problem tummies, Pear cut

Ball Gown

Fitted Bodice with Full Skirt

☑ Slender upper body Diamond Girls, Emerald cut, Pear cut

✗ Very petite, Heart cut, Princess cut

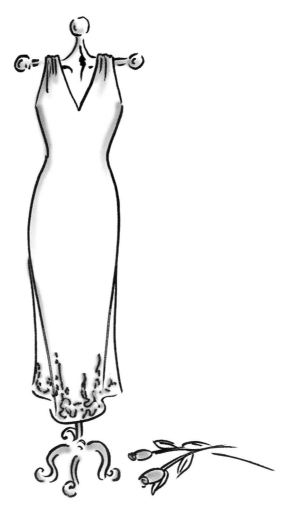

Sheath

Fits Close Following the Body's Natural Curves

- ☑ Slender figures, Emerald cut
- ☒ Not as good for all other Diamond Girls

Princess

Like an A-Line but with Seams from the Middle of the Bust to the Hips

- ☑ Short waists, Pear cut
- ⊗ Thick waists, Princess cut

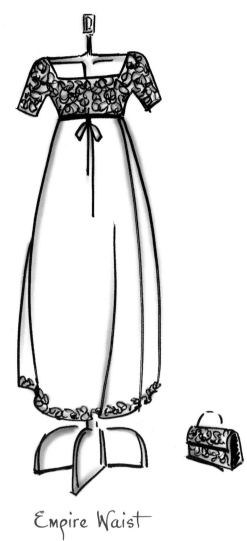

Empire Waist

Tiny Bodice with High Waist and Flared Skirt

☑ Thick waist, Princess cut, Emerald cut

☒ Full hips, Thin waists, Pear cut

Drop Waist

Like a Ball Gown but Waist Hits Below Belly Button

☑ *Tiny waists, Heart shape*

☒ *Narrow shoulders, Long waist, Emerald cut*

A-Line

Fitted Through the Torso, the Skirt Is Slightly Flared Like an "A"

☑ Most Diamond Girls

⊗ For almost no one

Match the Girl to the Gown

Pear

Heart

Emerald

Princess

Basque

Ball Gown

Sheath

Princess

Empire

Drop

A-Line

BRIDAL BENCHMARKS

As the reality of taking your measurements once a week begins to sink in, we will concede that if that seems too often, you certainly can take them bimonthly, but you *need* to take them. Your measurements, more than your weight, will really tell you if you are on track. In addition to our measurements, we all have our own unique ways to gauge if we are losing weight or if our body is changing. Most brides we asked use their old, faithful blue jeans as the truest sign of weight loss or gain. Oh no! More blue-jean torture! I know one woman who has three pairs of jeans that she uses as her barometer: thin, natural, and premenstrual. She knows that if she's not comfortable in her PMS jeans, it's definitely time to reel it in. Find a marker that works for you, whether it is your jeans or a favorite dress. You may want to choose a dress with a line similar to that of your wedding gown. Clearly the best built-in bridal benchmark (say *that* ten times fast!) of how your body is changing will be when you try on your gown at your fittings. Generally, if you buy your dress six months before your wedding day, you will have four fittings. You will get measured at your first fitting, the day you choose your dress. Your second fitting is usually scheduled five months before your wedding day. The third fitting is ten weeks before and the final fitting is about a month before you get married. Even if you only have three months between the time you purchase your dress and the wedding, you will still have the same four fittings. Your second fitting will be two months to six weeks before your wedding, your third fitting about a month before the wedding, and the final fitting one week before the big day. Make sure you choose your shoes before your second fitting, as well as your bridal bra or bustier. This is very important because the hem of your dress will be altered to suit your wedding shoes and a simple bra change can cause your gown to fit improperly.

Use these fittings to make sure you can move comfortably in your gown and gauge how your body is changing. Make sure that the fabric doesn't pull, bunch, or pucker. Be aware that most bridal salons charge a fee if you lose more that 10 pounds because they will have to do additional alterations. Hey, if that happens, consider it the best check you'll ever have to write.

Suzanne

If the Gown Fits, Wear It

At my second-to-last fitting, I did have to have my dress taken in. I felt so great about it. This was a real bridal benchmark for me and the experience actually rejuvenated my commitment to the Wedding Workout. I don't know how happy the designer was about it, but I left there wearing a perma-smile that lasted all day.

Trying on bridal gowns can be an exciting but uncomfortable experience. Most salons require an appointment. I showed up for my first appointment with a friend and was greeted by two very nice salesladies. I checked out all the dresses and chose a few that I liked. The two women then whisked me off to a dressing room with a pedestal in it. I was then asked to strip down to my underwear while they were in the room. I was under the spotlight again, except this time it felt more like a prison searchlight. I have never been much of an exhibitionist, so I was a little freaked out. Not to mention, I heard my mother's voice echoing in my head, "You should have worn your good underwear . . . and not a thong." Feeling totally vulnerable, I divulged my bra size so the saleswomen could supply me with a bustier for trying on the dresses.

I know that these women see brides of all shapes and sizes, but for me that wasn't even a comfort. The dresses are commonly a size 6 or 8, which means they are either going to fit you or they are not. The humiliation continued. The saleswomen reassured me that any dress I chose would be fit to my specific measurements. Having to repeatedly get naked in front of a shop mirror and in front of strangers was a strong motivator for me to get in shape.

I initially thought I wanted a sleeveless, boat-neck, A-line dress. After trying on a few, I decided that the style made me look stocky and less feminine. The emphasis the style put on my arms was not flattering. I did, however, conclude that the A-line was perfect for my Pear-cut body type. I have hips and didn't want to overemphasize that area, which is why the A-line is perfect for me.

A month later when I finally made a decision on a dress, I had to have my measurements taken. Hello, trauma! There is nothing like actually hearing your true measurements and having to face the truth that those numbers aren't 36-24-36. The saleswoman actually told me not to look at my details because they increased the measurements slightly to accommodate changes. Of course I peeked and was mortified. I was sure there was a mistake, and after forcing her to measure certain areas (such as my rear) again, I realized I needed to get a comprehensive fitness and eating plan into motion. This is the plan that Tracy helped me put into action, turning my initial pain into one of the greatest accomplishments of my life. Thus began the Wedding Workout! ↝

3

The Wedding Workout

At this point you should be getting excited about all of the possibilities in your life as you become the bride you want to be, and we also hope that you are now eagerly anticipating the Wedding Workout. As you approach this section first, we would like you to take just a moment to reflect on all the wonderful elements that make up the loving relationship you have created with your fiancé. Our assumption is that your relationship includes important essentials such as honesty, communication, support, humor, respect, independence, balance, and compromise. Most likely, the precise combination of all of these features is what made you fall madly in love with your man and absolutely convinced you that this guy is the one. The choice you make in a partner is one of the most important choices you will make in your lifetime. You have chosen him because your relationship embraces the elements you feel will provide you with a strong, healthy, thriving relationship worthy of "I do!" While some qualities may be more important to you than others, it is the *combination* of your fiancé's qualities that makes you certain that he is the one. Now, imagine for a brief moment what you would do if your guy was missing any one of these important qualities. If this were true, you might still be in Singleville looking for the right man to share your life with!

Like your love relationship, the Wedding Workout is also composed of various components necessary to successfully alter your body composition and achieve your desired results. This time, however, the relationship is between you and yourself! The components provide you with everything you need to make this relationship a successful one; however, if you choose to leave out any one of them, we can promise that you will sacrifice some measure of success. You must commit (just like your wedding vows) to the program and embrace each component wholeheartedly, regardless of your strengths and weaknesses. We will tell you what you need to do, but you are ultimately responsible for doing it!

THE FOUR WEDDING WORKOUT ESSENTIALS

The overall goal of the Wedding Workout is to help you increase your flexibility and improve your posture while losing fat, creating lean muscle, and becoming a stunningly beautiful bride who is in the best shape of her life!

As in your relationship with your fiancé, you may prefer or be more successful in one of these areas than in others. Still, you cannot let a weakness in one area get the best of you. For example, say you go through the blood, sweat, and

> **THE FOUR KEY COMPONENTS OF THE WEDDING WORKOUT ARE:**
>
> 1. Flexibility and posture
> 2. Cardiorespiratory activity
> 3. Musculoskeletal training
> 4. Healthy eating

tears of doing your prescribed cardiorespiratory activity, but you continue to eat horribly. What would be the point? The awesome effort behind your blood, sweat, and tears would be wasted on chocolate éclairs and ice cream. Not to mention you would most likely find yourself not changing at all, changing only slightly, reaching plateaus, or just giving up and feeling frustrated.

Instead, you must always incorporate all of the components of the Wedding Workout and think in terms of the big picture. By doing so, the strength you build in one area will only make you more determined to pick up the slack in the areas where you are not as strong. For example, you will use the confidence and power you gain from consistently doing your cardio to inspire you to eat well. You won't even care about an éclair! You will care about how confident and good you feel! In turn, the strength and self-trust you gain from eating with discipline will inspire you to do more cardio. The components will influence each other and you will be able to say to yourself, "Hey! I am *really* doing this!" Only then can you add that newfound confidence to your emotional trousseau.

We've seen so many people try to do one component of the Wedding Workout without the others and they never achieve what they really want. You have a choice here to make a change. If you are going to do it, do it! We encourage you to really go for it. Not "kind of," not "sort of," but for REAL. How inspiring is that! How uninspiring is kind of, sort of? After all, you don't "kind of" want to get married, now do you? What if your fiancé "sort of" wanted to tie the knot? Think about it! You have both agreed to show up at the ceremony because you both really want to get married. You are both really going to do it. After all, weddings are serious business. People are going to come from far and wide to witness this profound act of commitment taking place. Approach the four components with the same conviction, and you *will* see a change!

Now, let's take a look at each component.

Flexibility and Posture

By *flexibility* we mean stretching your muscles thoroughly to increase your range of motion and energy flow along with your physical and mental well-being. All too often flexibility is overlooked as an important part of having a healthy body. Through improving your flexibility, you can learn to release tension and tightness. You will feel elongated and agile as though you are not only a bride, but also the lead ballerina in *The Nutcracker*!

By *posture* we mean the way you carry yourself. Do you shrug from the world or stand up to it? The way you stand speaks volumes about the inner you. Did you know that posture is synonymous with attitude?

Cardiorespiratory Activity

By *cardiorespiratory activity* we mean any fitness activity that requires movement and increases your heart rate, such as walking, cycling, riding a stationary bike, running outdoors or on a treadmill, hiking, using a StairMaster or the Precor machine, swimming, taking an aerobics class, or kickboxing. In other words, Ms.

> ## Suzanne
>
> I really enjoy each component of the Wedding Workout. I find that I am usually very motivated to strength-train and work on my flexibility. However, healthy eating and cardio require more discipline for me. Still, I see the combination is what really gets me in shape. e⌒

Bride-to-be, let's get moving!!! When you are active, your muscles need more energy than when they are at rest. They rely on energy acquired from food already stored as calories in your body. Often these calories are stored as fat. Therefore, the main purpose of your cardiorespiratory workout regimen will be to decrease your stored body fat by mobilizing and utilizing excess calories. Other benefits include reduced blood pressure as well as decreased anxiety, tension, and depression that may be sneaking up on you in this rather hectic and exciting time.

Musculoskeletal Training

By *musculoskeletal training* we mean resistance or weight training with free weights in order to create or maintain muscle mass while building strength and definition. Did you know that muscle not only weighs more than fat, but it also burns calories faster than fat does? As a result of creating muscle, you will not only look better and feel stronger, but you will also be burning more calories. Also, weight training will help to improve your posture and maintain or increase your bone density, which will help prevent osteoporosis.

Healthy Eating

By *healthy eating* you can bet we do not mean DIET or DEPRIVATION!!!! We do mean eating fresh, healthy foods with high nutritional value and making better food choices while also adopting better habits. It is important that you eat consistently throughout the day in order to keep your body fueled at all times and your metabolism running. We want you to learn about the foods that are right for you. And finally, we definitely mean thinking of food as your friend, not your enemy. Now that we've introduced you to the four components, let's see how they relate to your metabolism.

MEET YOUR METABOLISM

Your metabolism is the rate at which energy stored in your cells is used to fuel your body. The energy comes from the food you eat and is represented as calories. Did you know that at rest, without doing a single thing, your body uses energy just for you to live? It may seem quite obvious, but have you ever really thought about it? Your body uses energy for your heart to beat, for your lungs to breathe, to support your muscle tone, and for all body processes.

The minimum number of calories you need to sustain life at rest is referred to as your basal metabolic rate (BMR). We like to refer to it as your resting metabolic rate, or RMR. Your RMR usually accounts for about 65 to 75 percent of your daily energy expenditure. We know that a lot of you run the other way when confronted with numbers and equations about your body. So, don't turn that page (yet). Did you know that children have a higher RMR because they have more lean body mass? So do pregnant women. Fevers can raise your RMR and so can stress, which is why a lot of brides-to-be lose weight very close to the big day. Fasting, starvation, and malnutrition lower your RMR, so it is no wonder that if you eat only a frozen yogurt and an apple all day long you probably won't lose weight. Sound familiar? Body type can also be a contributing factor to your RMR. Depending what body type you are, your RMR will vary. Remember our Diamond Girls? Emerald is tall and thin, indicating that she has a higher RMR than other Diamond Girls. Emerald is the kind of gal we envy, born with an RMR that the rest of us would sell our souls for. Let's say that Emerald and Pear go to the same bridal shower tea and scarf down the exact same number of tea sandwiches and scones with clotted cream. Yum! Each woman, however, will metabolize the same food differently. Because Emerald's RMR is higher, Pear will have to work harder to make sure that the clotted cream doesn't end up as added cushion when she sits down.

If you are a Pear, Heart, or Princess . . . never fear. The exciting news is that you *can* alter your metabolism by how much exercise you do, how much muscle or lean body mass you have, and how you eat. And, in turn, you affect both your weight and fitness level. We refer to this as your active metabolic rate, or AMR. So, if Emerald sits on the couch all day, but Pear does her Wedding Workout, Pear can bring her AMR up to what Emerald's RMR is!

Here's an easy way for you to calculate your resting metabolic rate:

RMR = body weight in lbs. x 10 kcal/lb.

For example, if Pear weighs 130 pounds, she would multiply her weight by 10, thus getting 1,300. This is her RMR, the calories her body needs to function at rest. This represents only how much she burns at rest and does not account for how much she burns during daily prewedding activities. To figure her AMR, she would need to use the following calculation:

$$1,300 \ (\text{RMR}) \div 2 = 650$$

(This number represents her daily basic caloric expenditure.)

$$\text{AMR} = 650 + 1,300 \ (\text{RMR}) = 1,950$$

Thus 1,950 represents Pear's active metabolic rate before she does her Wedding Workout. For every 30 minutes of cardiorespiratory exercise, Pear gets to add 200 to 300 calories to her AMR. So, if Pear runs for 30 minutes on a given day, her AMR will be roughly 2,250 calories. Whoa! That doesn't mean that she can eat 2,250 calories and lose weight. I wish! From her total AMR, Pear needs to create a deficit in order to lose weight and then maintain that weight loss. The best way for her to do this is to follow this calculation:

$$2,250 \ (\text{AMR}) \times 20\% = 450 \ (\text{calorie deficit})$$

So, Pear will have to cut back by 450 calories and eat roughly 1,800 calories each day. By reducing her intake while increasing her expenditure, Pear will lose weight.

To get a clear picture, we want you to imagine a four-carat diamond as the engine providing the power to run your body. Now, imagine converting the four-carat diamond engine into an eight-carat diamond engine in order to do the same job. The eight-carat diamond would have more density, power, and shine to get the same job done a lot more efficiently. By combining the four components of the Wedding Workout, you will convert your four-carat engine into an eight-carat diamond machine! To better understand how the Wedding Workout components influence each other and affect your metabolism, think about the following:

1. When you eat healthy, you increase the amount of energy you have for cardiorespiratory activities.

2. When you are active in cardiorespiratory activities and musculoskeletal training, you burn more stored calories, decrease your body fat, and increase muscle mass.

3. When you have more muscle, you burn more calories at rest, so you can eat more.

4. When you utilize more calories and eat more calories (but fewer than you utilize), you lose weight and increase your metabolism. You then have extra energy to engage in more cardiorespiratory activities and musculo-skeletal training.

See! All of the components are crucial for optional results.

SETTING UP A SCHEDULE

Your Wedding Workout schedule may depend on many factors, including the length of your engagement, how far along in your engagement you are when you acquire this book, what your specific fitness goals are, and just how much time you see this bride-to-be realistically being willing or able to commit. Just as an engagement period prepares you for marriage, so should you take time to mentally prepare before you begin your Wedding Workout regimen. This may mean three days or three weeks. Do whatever you have to do in order to get ready and prepare yourself to dig deep inside yourself to face the challenge that lies before you. I always tell my clients, "Don't start until you are mentally ready—and you will know when you are ready!"

Tracy

Whenever I decide to get in top shape, a Sunday night grocery store spree is undoubtedly my most helpful mental preparation ritual. We'll discuss this again in chapter 8, but for now just consider it a great motivator and a way to rid yourself of the Sunday back-to-work blues.

As I mentioned before, part of being mentally prepared is setting specific goals about what you want to achieve. These goals should be realistic and within reach. They can be about more than just decreasing a number on a scale. Perhaps they will have something to do with shifting your perspective on exercise. For example, if you usually can eat well and exercise for, say, only a month at a time before falling off the wagon (or treadmill), know that about yourself. It's okay! You can always get back on the wagon (or treadmill)! Simply being aware of your limitations sometimes enables you to change them. In this case, before you started, you would take time to mentally prepare to attempt six weeks instead of your usual four. Whatever you do, avoid setting up unrealistic goals and expectations for yourself. Remember, we only want to create new healthy habits and happiness here, not discouraging cycles of despair. This is an exciting time, not a time to beat yourself up for what you didn't do! Remember, understanding any challenge in life is a courageous, positive thing. The challenge is only here for you to conquer it, not for it to conquer you.

I have many clients who are so excited to start a new program that they almost always go overboard with enthusiasm and inevitably burn out, quit, or get discouraged when the excitement wears off. Remember that like your marriage, your health requires a commitment from you for the long haul. It is not a one-day deal or even a one-month deal. You don't want to be a burnout bride, so you must pace yourself!!!

I know that as a trainer I love to exercise and eat healthy as much as I love anything in the whole world. Still, as much as I love it, it certainly is not always easy for me. Sometimes, in fact, it is quite the opposite. Staying in shape all year is a full-time job and there are always ebbs and flows. In my years of training I have learned there is no such thing as always eating well or always being in perfect shape. There are times when I am in better shape than others. I simply can't stay in top shape all the time, nor would I want to because I would surely miss out on some of the greatest joys in life (cookies, chocolate, popcorn)! I've learned that I can usually train for about six weeks at a time before my body needs to rest, have a cookie, and take some time off. It has taken me a while, but I have finally learned how to pace myself so that I can maintain my fitness level longer. Therefore, whether you are a "new to exercise" bride-to-be, an "I hate exercise" bride-to-be, an "I love exercise" bride-to-be, an "I have to lose 10 pounds" bride-to-be, or an "I'm ready to go" bride-to-be, you will need to pace yourself with regard to your wedding date. You must trust that your rest days are as beneficial to your body as your workout days. If you are excited about getting on the plan, I appreciate your enthusiasm. Pace yourself and you will benefit more in the long run! ☞

By mentally ready we mean knowing exactly what it is you would like to accomplish. You must acknowledge that certain behaviors are going to have to change and you must be ready to let go of them. At the same time, new behaviors that may require time and energy need to be incorporated into your life. If really taking care of yourself weren't so time consuming, more people would be doing it! Ask yourself if you have factored workouts, cooking, and grocery shopping into your already hectic schedule. How do you plan to fit everything in? We suggest booking your workouts in your date book. "X-out" the time you need each day and shuffle your other plans around exercise.

THE WEDDING WORKOUT CYCLES

Every bride has a different length of engagement. Some can be as long as two years and some can be as short as a week. In order to accommodate as many brides as possible, we have decided to provide a six-month program broken down into 4 six-week cycles (see page 51). Just as the thought of saying "I do" can be overwhelming, so can the thought of doing anything physically challenging for six months. Our hope is that the six-week cycles will seem less daunting and will allow you the flexibility of beginning the program when you want to. Here's how the cycles work.

- CYCLE 1, COMMITMENT CYCLE: Six months, 24 weeks—I'm ready for the long haul!
- CYCLE 2, PLEDGE CYCLE: Four-and-a-half months, 18 weeks—I think I can, I think I can!
- CYCLE 3, VOW CYCLE: Three months, 12 weeks—Am I married yet?
- CYCLE 4, DEVOTION CYCLE: Six weeks—This is it! I do or die!

Each six-week cycle represents a different level of exercise intensity and duration. Both your cardiorespiratory and musculoskeletal training sessions will increase in difficulty relative to the nearness of your wedding day. Think of the

CYCLE 1	CYCLE 2	CYCLE 3	CYCLE 4
6-MONTH COMMITMENT CYCLE	4.5-MONTH PLEDGE CYCLE	3-MONTH VOW CYCLE	6–WEEK DEVOTION CYCLE
6-Month Checklist	**4.5-Month Checklist**	**3-Month Checklist**	**6-Week Checklist**
☐ Select a date and location	☐ Register for gifts	☐ Discuss service with officiant	☐ Apply for marriage license
☐ 20 to 25 minutes of cardio	☐ Finalize guest list	☐ 30 to 35 minutes of cardio training	☐ 40 minutes of cardio
☐ Moderate exercise intensity	☐ 25 to 30 minutes of cardio	☐ Moderate, interval, and high-intensity mix	☐ Interval and high-intensity training
☐ Order your dress	☐ Moderate and interval training	☐ Schedule rehearsal dinner	☐ Confirm rehearsal dinner
☐ Choose your bridesmaids	☐ Order invitations and hire calligrapher	☐ Schedule dress fittings	☐ Pick up wedding bands
☐ 2 exercises for each body part	☐ Plan honeymoon	☐ Choose ceremony readings	☐ Organize trousseau
☐ 1 and 2 wedding bell levels	☐ 2 exercises for each body part	☐ 2 exercises for each body part	☐ 2 exercises for each body part
☐ Set from each of the push-up exercises	☐ Set from each of the push-up exercises	☐ Set from each of the push-up exercises	☐ Set from each of the push-up exercises
☐ Complete the guest list	☐ 1 and 2 wedding bell levels	☐ 1, 2, and 3 wedding bell levels	☐ 2 and 3 wedding bell levels
☐ Book the florist, caterer, and photographer	☐ Choose wedding favors and bridal party gifts	☐ Order wedding bands	☐ Have test makeup and hairstyle done
☐ Book the band or disc jockey	☐ Select groom's attire	☐ Buy dress accessories	☐ Give idea list to photographer and videographer
	☐ Select groomsmen's and bridesmaids' attire	☐ Discuss menus with caterer	

Wedding Workout as a fitness road you have set out on that will lead you to the chapel. However, this road is not flat; it is a hill that you must climb in order to meet your goals and your fiancé at the top.

If you want to start out easy and give yourself the most time to get in shape, we recommend starting six months out in cycle 1. Because you have so much time, this is an easier climb, but realize you have longer to go and I want you to focus on staying the course. If you are already in pretty good shape and just want to lose a few pounds or tone up, you could start the program in cycle 2. You will, however, have to start at a higher intensity level to meet your goals than if you had the benefit of more time. If you don't start the Wedding Workout until cycle 4 or even four weeks before your wedding, you will have to start with the most intense workouts, but your time on the program before the big day will be less. Trust me, though; you can still accomplish a lot in a few weeks. You will just have to add some serious focus and a load of discipline in that bridal backpack you'll be carrying up Matrimony Mountain. We guarantee, though, that whichever cycle you choose to begin in, you'll feel amazing when you get to the top.

What if you want to start the program five months before your big day? No problem. You can enter a cycle in the middle, but we want you to complete that cycle before you move on to the next cycle. For example, if you started the program five months out, you would be starting in cycle 1 with two weeks left. You might take those two weeks to start slowly before diving into cycle 2, where you will be required to step up the intensity of your workouts. You could also wait, mentally prepare, and begin the program at cycle 2. Once again, be aware that wherever you start will determine how aggressively you will have to implement the program.

After completing each cycle, you are encouraged to take at least two days off to breathe, relax, and reward yourself for your efforts before starting your next cycle. Your days off may include a trip to the spa, a movie with a large popcorn, or taking a salsa dance class for fun. I'm not telling you to throw your progress to the wind, but do enjoy yourself. While we would like you to enjoy the breaks between cycles, if doing so makes you feel like you might get off track, then it is perfectly fine for you to continue the program without a break. We just don't want you to burn out, especially if you are starting in cycle 1.

With regard to weight loss, the cycles are designed to prevent you from taking any drastic measures to try to lose 10 pounds in a week. This would not be good! We really want you to do it safely and gradually so you can keep it off. If you have 20 or more pounds to lose, enter the Wedding Workout in cycle 1 and let's go for it! You need to allow yourself as much time as possible to safely reach your goals. Your goal will be to lose about 2 to 3 pounds the first week, followed by 1 to 2 pounds each week thereafter. If you have 15 or more pounds to lose, you should begin in cycle 1, 2, or 3, aiming to lose 1 to 2 pounds the first week, also followed by 1 to 2 pounds each week thereafter. If you have only 10 pounds to lose, you should start in cycle 3 or 4, with the goal of losing 1 pound the first week, followed by 1 pound each week thereafter. No matter how much weight you are trying to shed or even if you don't have any weight to lose, start the Wedding Workout whenever you feel like getting into better shape and getting more out of your life! Our goal is for fitness and health to become a part of your everyday life. We really don't want you future brides to use this workout solely for your wedding and then forget it! But we also want to encourage you to strive for balance, set realistic goals, and maintain a proper, healthy perspective.

MAKING THE POSITIVE CHOICE

If you are on page 54 of *The Wedding Workout,* then clearly, you are a bride-to-be who really wants to change your life and appearance. For that we applaud you! We have helped many brides who truly believed they were stuck in their preengaged bodies, only to see them happily slim down and shape up. We know that you, too, can change your body, if you commit. Sadly, we see many women resign themselves to being unhappy in their bodies and always wishing they looked different. They don't realize or believe they can truly make a choice to do something about how they feel. Our view is that it is going to be hard no matter what choice you make. You can make the passive decision to stay the same or the active decision to strive for something more.

Whatever your struggles with food, exercise, and self-image may be, you can make a very powerful, active choice and initiate a change. Just like getting married, the decision to finally get up and do it can be very rewarding and motivating in and of itself. Now it is time to put intention into action. You must continually invest yourself in the commitment to your health. After all, the best investment you can ever make is the investment you make in yourself. Invest, reinvest, invest and reinvest! The time is *now!* Tape your ideal body picture to your bathroom mirror, your refrigerator, and your dashboard. Put it everywhere so you will constantly be reminded of what you want in your life. Rent movies like *Rocky, Rudy, Without Limits, Flashdance,* and even *Charlie's Angels*. They will remind you about the power of hard work and victory! Get inspired about your body and being active! Create your own soundtrack to use while exercising. Whatever you do, be proud of the struggle you have chosen. All you ever do in life is try! Doing something about your health is going to be a lot more exciting than sitting around feeling

SAMPLE CHART OF NEGATIVE CHOICES / POSITIVE CHOICES

NEGATIVE CHOICE	POSITIVE CHOICE
I hate my body.	I can improve my body if I choose.
I ate a brownie; I'm fat.	Today is a new day. I'm going to try to stay on my plan.
Other women look better than me.	I appreciate other women and that we are unique and beautiful.

unfulfilled, complacent, and in pain while doing nothing about it. Congratulations! You have made the active, positive choice. Positive and negative choices are always present (see preceding chart). Keep making the positive choice! Stay focused on the positive choice. Don't stray off track. We are certain you will be capable of achieving more than you ever thought possible!

DETERMINING YOUR GOALS

A goal is an intention, a purpose, an objective—something to strive for in your life. It may take some time and some soul searching, but deciding what you want out of the Wedding Workout is the first step in making the changes that will give you the body you want.

Sometimes a goal is the only thing you have to hold on to when you can't see immediate results. Maybe you've never been great at setting goals. If getting ready for your wedding and starting an incredible new period in your life doesn't make you want to set goals, then what will? Think about the alternatives. Do you really want to look back at your wedding photos and regret that you didn't look your best on your wedding day?

Now that you have decided to set some goals, write them down, make it official. We've included a journal page for you to record these goals in preparation for your new workout regimen. (See page 57.) We can assure you that making a commitment is sometimes the only thing that will get you up in the morning and keep you going. Be bold. Write down a goal even if some little voice inside of you tells you that it could never happen. Writing out your goal will inspire you, raise your energy level, and most of all, help you believe in yourself. Remember that your life is up to you. No one else is going to do it for you. Having goals will provide you with a greater sense of well-being and purpose, and the goals will keep you focused despite all of life's distractions. Remember that you only get to experience this life, this day, this hour, this moment but once! Life is a gift and the only time you can really experience is *now*!

Now that you are getting out your pen, it is important that you clarify what your goals for your Wedding Workout will be. Do you want to lose weight? If so, how much? Are you concerned about toning your arms and back? Are you aiming at getting in your best shape ever? Is your wedding day a catalyst for you to simply increase your exercise? Do you have a particular pair of old blue jeans you want to pull on again? How about feeling better? Why have you chosen this time to make a change? Is this a short-term commitment or a lifelong one?

Congratulations! Just having a goal is a step in the right direction. Change is always a process and it rarely includes perfection, so be sure to include some realistic, easy-to-achieve goals and graduate to the more ambitious ones. If

My Goals

thinking in terms of the long haul is too much for you, set daily or weekly goals. That way you can celebrate the victory of accomplishment a lot more often. It is important to achieve smaller goals along the way, not just to reach one stunning goal at journey's end.

Once you have written your goals down, it won't be quite as easy to disregard them. You will know deep down when you are not honoring your deepest desires. Don't be afraid to shoot high on your list. Think about what you really want. Have the courage to own what you really want no matter how far-fetched it may seem right now. You may soon surprise yourself by checking off your initial goals and creating new ones. You may never know what you can do unless you reach for it, or in this case, run, stretch, eat well, and exercise for it!

4

The Flexible and Statuesque Bride

Okay. Level with us here. Are you an uptight bride-to-be? Now, that can't be fun. We encourage you never to underestimate the power of the stretch! For this reason, we've chosen to start the Wedding Workout with the flexibility training section because flexibility is a vital component of any balanced fitness program. Yet it is often the most overlooked. By flexibility training, we don't just mean going through the motions of performing a few simple stretches. We mean really working at your stretches like an art form to ultimately increase your joints' abilities to move through a full range of motion. Only then will you truly benefit from all that flexibility has to offer.

> **Tracy**
>
> I used to have the tightest muscles west of the Mississippi. But since I've discovered my flexible side, I definitely have more fun in my workouts and in my life. ❧

As you approach the Wedding Workout, we encourage you to view flexibility as the core component that will tie your cardiorespiratory and musculoskeletal resistance-training sessions together. Additionally, it will help to greatly improve your posture. It is vital to maintaining mobility and agility as you grow older. After all, wouldn't you still like to be playing naked circus with your husband fifty years down the road? Trust us. There is nothing better than a lean, healthy body, which is not only strong but flexible. As you become a more flexible bride-to-be, it will become easier for you to move and you will exert less energy. This will then increase both your cardiorespiratory and musculoskeletal performance levels. Also, your increased range of motion will decrease resistance in your muscles, and your chances of hyperextending or injuring them will diminish. Your muscles will become more limber and balanced, helping to relieve soreness after exercise as well as reducing any lower-back pain you may have.

Like anything worth having in life, flexibility is something you must work at. Unless you are genetically blessed and ready for the Cirque du Soleil, you will most likely not find yourself folding up like a pretzel overnight. Flexibility takes time and consistency, but we assure you it can be improved. Don't think in terms of a quick 5-second stretch. Instead, take at least 30 seconds or more per stretch and really experience each one. Focus on your breathing and go as far as you can into each stretch before eliciting any pain. Use this time for you. Relax, breathe, and allow yourself to really be in each stretch. Feel your muscles elongate. Get inside of them and be aware of how your body is working from the inside out. Finally, take the awareness and centered feeling you get from improving your flexibility into other areas of your life, as well as into the other components of the Wedding Workout.

Tracy

When I was growing up, I had the flexibility of a piece of wood. But I was a really good athlete. I didn't understand how to become more flexible and how flexibility could add to my overall well-being. I thought only gymnasts were flexible and that flexibility was something they were born with. While some people are naturally able to lift their leg up over their head, I couldn't do a split if my life depended on it. When I finally left the weight room and starting doing more stretching and isometric exercises, I began to understand the power of flexibility. Instead of stretching for 10 seconds, I started to hold my stretches for 30 seconds, 45 seconds, and sometimes even longer. Also, I incorporated stretches throughout my workout, not just before and after. Immediately following a set, I would stretch the muscle I had just used. This gave my muscles time to lengthen and recover. The truth is that at first it was very painful and frustrating

continued on next page

for me to stretch for any length of time. I didn't think that I could ever get better at it, but I persevered. Within a year of focusing on stretching, I was able to do the splits. Who knew that a split could make someone so happy! That was cause for celebration. Now that I have increased flexibility, I realize that being more agile makes me feel stronger in everything I do—not to mention, it's really fun.

In *The Wedding Workout*, I've included many of my favorite Wedding Workout stretches. If you are familiar with yoga, you will recognize some of these. When you begin each stretch, it is important to inhale as you start and exhale as you push further into the stretch. You need to be really conscious of your breathing because it can literally help you push beyond your limit and take you further into a stretch. Don't push too hard, and when it feels good hold the stretch for as long as you like. Only go as fast or deep as the slowest part of you is willing to go. Try to stretch from your center, not just from the body part you're stretching. Make each stretch active and energized. You want to think of creating a line of energy, as if you have a live wire running through your limbs. You want to extend that energy and then relax it with the same intensity that you started with. Whatever your limits are when you begin, they will diminish with time and practice. You don't have to become a yogi or a trapeze artist to become an agile and flexible bride. If you think all this is hoopla, give it a little time and you will find yourself taking pride in deepening your stretches. Bet you never knew a stretch could offer such a powerful sense of accomplishment! ℮

SEATED STRETCHES

INNER-THIGH STRETCH

Bridal Benefits: I love this stretch because it is great for freeing up tension in my hips. It also improves circulation and energy flow through my legs, hips, and pelvic region. It increases flexibility in my inner-thigh, or adductor, muscles. It also helps to lengthen and strengthen my spine.

Sit on the floor with your legs bent and the soles of your feet touching. Lace your fingers and grasp your feet, pulling them in toward your groin as close as possible. Using your inner thighs, consciously press your knees toward the floor as you elongate your spine and pull your chest up and away from the floor. For a deeper stretch, use your elbows as weights and press them into your knees. Hold for 30 seconds.

CROSS-LEGGED HIP AND TRICEP STRETCH

Bridal Benefits: This stretch is great because it simultaneously releases tension in my shoulders and triceps as well as my hips and bottom. During this stretch, I concentrate a lot on keeping my chest lifted and my back as flat as I can get it. This helps my posture and increases the circulation between my upper and lower body. It gives me a full-body connected feeling fast!

Sit on the floor and cross your right leg over your left at the knee. Stretch your right arm straight up. Then bend your right elbow and place your palm on your back. Clasp your right elbow with your left hand to push your palm further down your back. Keeping your abdomen in and your chest lifted, press your flat back forward over your knees. Exhale smoothly. Hold for 30 seconds and then repeat on the other side.

DEEP QUAD STRETCH

Bridal Benefits: During this stretch, I can literally feel any tension in my lower back fully release. Not only has my lower back become more flexible with this stretch, but it has gotten a lot stronger. After a strong leg set, this is my favorite stretch for lengthening my quadriceps and hip flexors. Careful, though! It can be a rather intense stretch depending on how tight your quadriceps are.

Sit on your heels with your knees no more than hip-width apart. Place your hands on the floor, behind and to the sides of your ankles, with your fingertips facing forward. Contract your pelvis under and simultaneously try to lift your hips off your heels. Think of pulling your quadriceps toward you as you tip your tailbone under. Your hips will be lifting up as you pull your belly button toward your spine. Concentrate on bowing your chest open to the ceiling and feeling energy through each arm as you press your hips and chest away from the floor. For an even deeper stretch, maintain your alignment and slowly lower to your forearms and elbows. Hold for 30 seconds.

OPPOSITE HAND TO FOOT STRETCH

Bridal Benefits: This stretch is also great for increasing flexibility in both my quadriceps and hip flexors. I use it to improve my posture and my balance. This one can be challenging at first and can go very deep.

Kneel and bring your right foot out in front of your right knee in a lunge position. Place your left hand on the floor and with your right hand try to grab your left toe behind you. Keeping your chest up and back straight, press your hips and upper body forward as you pull your heel into your seat. As your upper body moves forward, be sure not to leave your bottom behind you. While pressing your hips toward the floor, keep your front knee directly under your chest. Hold for 30 seconds, then switch sides.

BALL STRETCH

Bridal Benefits: I love this stretch because it is very easy and effective. It greatly releases tension in my lower back. When I try to get my back as flat, flat, flat as I can, it feels as though someone is pulling me from each end of my spine. It gives me a very centered and connected feeling.

Lie on your back with your legs bent and both feet flat on the floor. Bring both knees in toward your chest. Clasp the knees with both hands and gently pull them into your chest. Press your hips down and flatten your shoulder blades deep down into the floor. This will round your chest a little toward the ceiling. Keep your chin down and your head on the floor. You want to lengthen your back. Think of it as pulling your torso long and flat. Hold for 30 seconds.

BALL STRETCH NUMBER TWO

Bridal Benefits: This stretch includes all the great benefits of the ball stretch and additionally opens my hips while stretching the inner thighs and hamstrings. It's fun! I usually feel like a little space invader turned upside down.

For a deeper stretch, take the knees to the sides of your chest and make your calves vertical, with your heels directly over your knees and the soles of your feet facing the ceiling. Clasp the insides of your feet and pull your feet straight down as though you are going to put your knees on the floor. Hold for 30 seconds.

STRAIGHT LEG STRETCH

Bridal Benefits: This stretch is one of my favorites, but it is also the one that is most difficult for me. While it has been excellent for increasing the flexibility in my hamstrings and inner thighs, it has also been the most challenging in terms of working on my posture. It took me a long time to get my back flat, and some days I really have a hard time keeping it there.

Kneel, keeping your knees hip-width apart. Keeping your left bottom directly over your left knee and using your hands for support, slide your right leg straight in front of you as you rest on your heel. Inhale and round your back like a cat; exhale

and try to pull your back out flat like a tabletop. Think of reaching your forehead over your toe and lengthen your back as far as you can. Keep your hips even and square. Hold for 30 seconds before switching sides. For a deeper stretch, pull your front toes toward you as you keep rotating your back hip forward.

STRAIGHT LEG STRETCH NUMBER TWO

Bridal Benefits: Brides-to-be, are you ready for this one? We are now going to really work on your flexibility by continuing your straight leg stretch into a split toward the floor. If you are anything like me, it may take you a full year or more to get your hips all the way down. Maybe by your first wedding anniversary!

To begin, use your arm strength and hands for support as you ever so slowly slide your heel away from you. Keep your hips square at all times. Try not to let your sliding-leg hip fall back behind the other. By all means take your time and do not worry about how far you get down. Who cares! Remember to keep your back flat, your chest up, and your hips even so that your torso faces straight ahead. If your hips begin to rotate open, stop. This is your furthest point from which to build on. Good luck getting to the floor. Touching is an exhilarating and worthwhile feeling! If you can already touch, hooray! We know both you and your fiancé must be thrilled!

DEEP SIDE STRETCH

Bridal Benefits: I love this stretch, because it makes me feel pretty and feminine and graceful and willowy and elegant! I just love it! When we do this stretch in class, you can just feel the room turn into a Bob Fosse dance production! Not only do I feel beautiful while I'm doing this stretch, but my body feels completely unrestricted after it. My rib cage and chest feel open and expanded, while my spine, arms, and sides feel entirely elongated!

Kneel, keeping your knees hip-width apart. Contract your pelvis under and extend your right leg straight out from your right hip. Point your right toe and try to touch it to the floor. If you can, even better. With your left arm, reach up over your head and use your right hand to balance yourself on your right leg. Turn your chin toward your left shoulder, opening your rib cage toward the ceiling. Hold for 30 seconds, then switch sides.

COBRA

Bridal Benefits: This isn't my favorite stretch as far as comfort is concerned, but the benefits are fantastic. This is a great stretch to do following your abdominal sets. It is a super lower-back opener and chest opener, and really helps to release tension in the spine. While being a great abdominal stretch, the Cobra also helps strengthen your back. Also, if you extend your bottom teeth and jut your chin forward, you really stretch your throat and neck, which feels great. Give it a try. This stretch may turn out to be your favorite.

Lie facedown on the floor, with your hands placed beneath your shoulders alongside your chest. If you want an easier stretch, place your hands farther forward. For a more difficult stretch, place your hands farther back, near your bottom rib. Think of gently tipping your pelvis into the floor as you contract your stomach and bottom. You want to think of your lower body as one unit while you press the tops of your feet into the floor. Try to think of pressing energy out through your toes. Inhale and press your palms into the floor while raising your upper body off the floor. Exhale and roll your shoulders away from the floor. You want to get a really strong curve without taking your belly button off the floor. Don't let your elbows flail to the sides; keep them close to your body. Try to create a reverse "C" shape and imagine touching your shoulder blades to your seat. This will really open up your chest and lengthen your spine. It's like doing a mini backbend. Hold for 30 seconds or more. When you're ready, slowly lower yourself back down to the floor.

CAMEL

Bridal Benefits: This one is good when you're in love because it opens your heart. I feel this is the most exhilarating stretch you can do. It is as though you can feel every cell in your body respond. This is a great stretch for opening the front of your body and increasing circulation. If you do this stretch after your stomach sets, you will feel a great energy release and lengthening sensation throughout your abdomen.

Kneel on the floor with your knees and feet hip-width apart. Point your toes straight back and press the tops of your feet into the floor. This will help to ground you. To begin, sit up tall, being mindful of your posture. Rest your palms on your buttocks. Tip your pelvis under, bow your chest up to the ceiling, and arch your back while reaching to clasp your heels. If at first you don't succeed, try it again with your toes curled under. By pulling off your heels and really straightening your arms, you will increase your curvature and your energy flow. You want to try to slowly drop your head back for the deepest stretch. Be careful because this stretch can make you feel a little light-headed. When you're starting out, you might want to practice arching back in this position before taking your hands all the way back to your heels. The best way to hold your heels is to place the fingertips inside the heels and the thumbs outside. Hold for at least 15 seconds and work your way up to 30.

For a more advanced version of this stretch that really lengthens your obliques, release one hand while continuing to hold on tight with the other hand. As you continue to press your hips forward, reach your fingertips up and over your head.

CHILD'S POSE

Bridal Benefits: This is a great, relaxing, comfortable position. It feels safe and nurturing, thus the name. This is a stretch that is wonderful to do after any exercise and it is a nice follow-up to your whole routine. We will be doing it primarily after push-ups because of its ability to really stretch out your chest and arms.

Kneel and sit on your heels. Lower your chest to your knees and reach your hands as far as you can in front of you. Once you're at your furthest point, turn your palms upward and press your forearms into the floor. Hold for 30 seconds or more. If you want a deeper stretch through your back, open your knees to the sides of your rib cage and try to drop your chest to the floor.

STANDING STRETCHES

FORWARD BEND STRETCH

Bridal Benefits: This stretch instantly lets you know how tight you are. It is always a great one to start with because it seems to wake up your entire body right away. You can relax or rest in this stretch, or if you are already warm, you can make it very challenging. This stretch really elongates my spine while stretching the entire back of my body. I use it particularly for my hamstrings. I tend to hold this position for well over a minute, and I have found that it is the most useful stretch for really increasing flexibility.

Stand with your feet parallel and hip-width apart. Inhale, exhale, and slide your hands down your legs and bend forward from your hips, not your stomach. Either clasp your hands around your legs or clasp your elbows and dangle. For a deeper stretch, rotate your hips up toward the ceiling while allowing the weight of your body to pull toward the floor. You should feel like your body is hanging from a hook on the back of a door. Hold for 30 seconds or more.

WIDE LEG DOWNWARD DOG STRETCH

Bridal Benefits: This is also a terrific overall body stretch! I feel it in my hamstrings, as well as my calves and Achilles tendon. I can feel the tension in my neck and shoulders dissipate, and I especially like the energizing feeling I get through my spine. It feels like liquid heat warming up my whole back.

Stand with your legs hip-width apart. As you inhale, place your hands on the floor in front of you and walk your feet behind you, placing them parallel to each other and 3 to 4 feet apart. Inhale, exhale, and press weight into your hands. With your

arms straight, drop your chest to the floor and push your hips behind you as far as you can. Think of tipping your hip or seat bones as high as you can up toward the ceiling. Keeping your back straight and flat, press your heels into the floor. Hold for 30 seconds.

STEEPLE SIDE STRETCH

Bridal Benefits: This is another one of those side stretches that just plain feels good. It is not as pretty as the Deep Side Stretch, but it is also great for lengthening your waistline, arms, and spine. If you put all your energy into it, this one can be quite challenging. Progress in this one is very noticeable! See how far you can get at first and have fun as you feel yourself dropping lower and lower.

Stand with your feet parallel and together. Squeeze your inner thighs together and tip your pelvis under, gently squeezing your gluteus and pulling your belly button toward your back. Inhale and reach both of your arms up behind your ears, lacing your fingers at the top. Press your index fingers together. Keep your arms tight and push energy through your fingertips.

Begin to wiggle from side to side, lifting your torso up and out of your hips. Imagine you are a tall building with a steeple and you're trying to reach the clouds above you. Exhale and draw a big arc with your fingertips as you drop as deep as you can to one side. Keep your chin up and your rib cage open toward the ceiling. Hold for 30 seconds, then switch sides.

STANDING QUADRICEPS STRETCH

Bridal Benefits: This is a very basic stretch for the quadriceps. It is quick and easy and doesn't require getting down on the floor. For this reason, it is useful if you are at all hurried going through your leg sets. In this stretch especially there is no room to hide poor posture. No matter how tired I am, I focus on keeping my head up, chest up, and shoulders back. After all, as my teacher used to say, "There is no use looking at the floor!" I find this stretch extremely beneficial for perfect posture practice.

Stand with your feet parallel (using a wall or countertop for support, if needed.) Use your right hand to pull your right foot up behind you. Bend your left knee slightly, tip your pelvis under, and pull your right knee toward the floor. Think of pulling backward with your quadriceps while squeezing forward with your pelvis. This will help to elongate your quadriceps. Hold for 30 seconds, then switch sides.

Hopefully, these stretches will be a catalyst to help you get reconnected with your body. By adding the Wedding Workout stretches to your everyday life, you can explore your body's capability and experience the empowerment that goes along with it. Remember, a flexible body can help teach you to be flexible in other areas of your life. Say good-bye to blocked energy and hello to a more open mind and greater self-acceptance. The flexibility you will gain will have you gliding out of bed in the morning, standing tall with an open, energized outlook on the world.

PERFECTING YOUR POSTURE

We've emphasized that stretching is a perfect arena within which to work on bettering your posture. While flexibility will be one aspect of your new, open attitude, posture is its direct complement. Often after my class, I see the same students who were zealously killing themselves to get in shape slump their shoulders and cave in their chests as soon as they walk out the door. This drives me crazy!!! They stand 2 inches shorter and look 5 pounds heavier than they actually are simply because their chests are collapsed in and their shoulders literally droop. As I kindly remind them to pull their shoulders back, I ask, "What is the point of a nice physique if you don't hold it up properly?" Imagine a beautiful Monet painting or an elegant Renoir being crumpled up and thrown in the garage. It most certainly would not have the same appeal, presence, or beauty as it does when properly hung in a gallery. Even the most beautiful works of art need to be exhibited correctly in order to sell or curators would be out of a job. It has been said that it's all in the presentation. Like a Monet or a Renoir, your body is a piece of art, and the way you present it is important! You are here to be admired and appreciated, and no one can do that if you are hunched over and closed off from the world. Always keep in mind that it is through your posture that you influence how others regard you and treat you. Your posture is a primary means by which you convey to others what is unique, special, and beautiful about you!

Think of all of the amazing things your body does for you. You only need to observe someone handicapped or sick for a few minutes to realize how often we completely take our health and our bodies for granted. Walking tall is simply a way to say you appreciate your body and your health, and that you like who you are.

Tracy

A few years ago, I had dinner with a boyfriend who seemed very agitated with me. I asked him what was wrong and to my surprise he replied, "You have horrible posture! You slumped your shoulders through the whole meal, and it drives me crazy!" Initially, I was appalled and hurt by his criticism. His criticism taught me he was not the guy for me; however, I learned an invaluable lesson from what he had said. I realized that my posture reflected something deeper inside of me—how I felt about myself.

The irony of the situation was that by criticizing me about my poor posture, my boyfriend showed me that it was my low self-esteem that had allowed me to be with someone that critical in the first place. Needless to say, I got rid of the boyfriend and I was determined to improve my posture. I practiced sitting up straight while driving my car, while at the hairdresser, while at the dinner table—everywhere! You couldn't catch me slumping anywhere but in a movie theater. As a result, I learned that poor posture doesn't always mean you have low self-esteem; it just makes you look like you do.

Suzanne

It's true. I've been working really hard on my posture. Still, I hate to admit it, but I'm one of the women who walks out of Tracy's class with my shoulders slumped. As soon as Tracy walks toward me, I immediately straighten up out of fear because she has told me that every time she sees me looking like the hunchback of Notre Dame's bride, I'm going to have to pay her money. That could be a whole dowry! My poor posture has plagued me as long as I can remember. Friends and family always comment on it and I always say, "I know, I'm working on it." What I really want to say is "Have you seen my sister's perfect posture? She went to finishing school while I went to tennis camp. I don't suppose you'd like to see my perfect forehand?" Seriously, as we've discussed, proper posture is a vital issue for any bride-to-be. Some women are lucky enough to have good posture or have developed it through exercise and dance. Others, like myself, have to work a little harder at it. For me, being conscious of it is half the battle. I've decided that from now until my wedding day, every time I catch my reflection in a mirror, I am going to stop and notice my posture. I feel really beautiful when I stand tall. How do I want to be standing on my wedding day? I want to focus on keeping my shoulders back with my chest held high, similar to the starting positions in the Wedding Workout. I know from my own experience that maintaining good posture is a constant struggle. But I also know that it will be a change whose benefits I can reap forever. ℮

Poor posture is really just a bad habit. The good news is that like most bad habits, poor posture can be changed. All it takes is some concentration, some practice, and a desire to look and feel more confident. I encourage you to become aware of your posture. I encourage you to consciously improve your posture so that you can radiate self-confidence and grace on your wedding day when all eyes will be on *you*. All my hard work on my posture really paid off on my wedding day. I felt great! The strength training for my shoulders and back allowed me to stand up straight in heels all night. I was especially mindful of my posture as I stepped into my dress. I knew that my gown was fitted for good posture and that if I slumped my shoulders for a second, the neckline and bodice of the dress would be comprised. I floated down the aisle, my head held high and my shoulders back, with an unprecedented sense of confidence. Your posture is *the* most important factor in how beautiful you will look in your wedding dress. No one wants to see a slumpy-shouldered bride. Now, begin to think about and observe your posture throughout the day. Begin to notice your posture in different situations. Practice sitting up straight, even if it feels uncomfortable at first.

The following exercises are great for increasing strength in your back and shoulders, which will also improve your posture. If you do them two to three times a week, you will surely walk down the aisle with absolute poise and confidence.

SEATED SCISSOR WALK

Bridal Benefits: Strengthens the muscles in the back and releases energy in the spine.

Sit in an armless chair holding a weight in each hand by your side. You can start with 2 pounds each and increase the weight as you gain strength. Inhale and breathe up into your chest while you lift your rib cage away from your hips. Keep your shoulders up and relax your shoulder blades down your back.

This will engage your perfect posture. The goal is to create length and movement in your spine, back, and shoulders. For maximum benefit, it is essential to maintain this posture during the exercise. Bring the weights in front of your chest. Walk your left arm by your left ear as you lower your right arm straight to the floor. Alternate walking your arms, 25 times per side. Keep your upper body perfectly still. Reach each fist as far away from the other as possible.

SEATED COMPRESSOR

Bridal Benefits: Strengthens the muscles in the back and releases energy in the spine.

Straddle an armless chair backward so that you can plant your back firmly against a wall. Hold a weight in each hand by your side, again starting with 2 pounds in each hand. Inhale and breathe up into your chest while you lift your rib cage away from your hips. Lift your

arms shoulder height and hold vertically in a field-goal position. With your back as flat as you can get it, rotate your forearms forward. Stop. Slowly return your arms back to the starting position. Repeat 8 to 15 times with or without weights.

BACK EXTENSION

Bridal Benefits: Kill two birds with one stone. Another great way to enhance your posture is the "T" Back Extension exercise provided in the "Back" section of chapter 6 (page 138).

As you move into the cardiorespiratory section, remember you are one fine statuesque bride-to-be. Take your proper posture habits into your cardio regimen—no slumping on the StairMaster. Don't forget to implement all of your Wedding Workout stretches before, during, and after your cardio and strength workouts. Be flexible and allow yourself to experience all the happiness you can during this time in your life. And always stand tall!

5

The Heart-Fit Bride

Now that you've learned the importance of being still, poised, and relaxed, it is time to learn the value of movement. As we explained earlier, the term *cardio-respiratory* refers to any aerobic activity that conditions your heart and lungs by increasing your oxygen intake. Unfortunately, the only way we know how to increase your heart and respiratory rate is to insist that you move. Too bad it can't happen lying down. At least not alone, anyway. If you move your body at a continuous pace over time, you will condition your heart and burn fat. Often, brides who desire toned arms simply lift weights and try to bypass doing any cardiovascular activity. Then they are frustrated and complain when they don't lose weight or see any muscle definition. This drives us bonkers! The bottom line is

Tracy

I was destined to become a fitness trainer. Since I was eleven years old, cardio has been a part of my life. That means for twenty years I've kept my heart, lungs, and body moving. If I calculate that I ran, hiked, or biked an average of four times a week, I can say I've engaged in cardio activity 4,160 times. That's a large number, probably only surpassed by the number of times I've brushed my teeth. Out of these 4,160 times, I honestly cannot recall a single time that I didn't feel better after doing my cardio. I guarantee that if you do it once, you'll know what I mean. I'm not saying that every cardio session will be easy, but I am saying that there is a 100 percent chance that you will feel good about yourself afterward. I know that cardiovascular exercise contributes to my overall well-being. And I just plain love it because it makes me feel good.

that to lose weight and get the lean, toned look you want, you must partake in cardiovascular exercise. It doesn't mean you can't burn fat simply by changing your diet and increasing your muscle mass, but cardio will increase the calories burned while you're at rest and raise your metabolism. You must exercise. We're sorry. There is simply no way around it. In other words, you have to forget being a couch potato and you must exercise aerobically to burn off the fat. If you are a sedentary bride-to-be, forgive us, but not moving is not an option. In fact, your mandatory cardiorespiratory prescription for the Wedding Workout includes three to five days of cardiovascular activity per week. No ifs, ands, or buts! Only I do's! I know that may sound like a lot, but the results will be worth it. In our experience, four cardio sessions a week is the best way to really see results. You will also be required to do three days of musculoskeletal training, but your primary weight loss is going to come from your die-hard commitment to your cardiorespiratory activity and eating well! If your goal is to lose weight, cardiovascular activity and healthy eating must be your priority! Therefore, if your time is limited, do not skip your cardio!!! Prioritize it over musculoskeletal training when scheduling your workouts. Once you have lost the excess weight, feel free to cut back a day on your cardio, with three sessions being the minimum. Perhaps then you'll want to add an extra day of strength training.

Tracy

You don't think that it is possible to love cardio? Just recently I began training a woman who had never run before or done any other type of cardiovascular activity. The first month she hated it—and me! But now she actually gets upset if she has to miss her cardio. She rides the bike, runs, and kickboxes, and she feels great! It is all a matter of determination, habit, discipline, and perspective! For me, cardio is my antidepressant of choice. Get excited and decide you are going to get moving! ↵

If you are currently inactive or you've never done much cardiovascular exercise, you are in for a real treat! Your body and mind are both going to feel so much better! You'll feel everything working. You may have to go through a stage where you will feel uncomfortable before you will consider yourself a "runner."

But when you feel discomfort, use it to motivate yourself instead of walking away from it. Be determined. And don't worry! No matter how difficult it may be at the beginning, we promise you it will get easier. You may even end up really liking it.

CHOOSING AN ACTIVITY

Fortunately, these days there are many aerobic activities to choose from. You can walk, swim, or ride an outdoor bike or a stationary one. You can run, kickbox, jump rope, or dance, use the VersaClimber, treadmill it, StairMaster it, Precor it (one of our favorites), or find some other kind of funky machine to get your heart rate up. And no, we do not mean your fiancé; that counts as an extracurricular activity. The possibilities are endless. You can exercise outdoors, indoors, with a group, with a partner, or alone. If you consult your local gym, you may even be able to find an aerobics or kickboxing class you could include in your Wedding Workout.

The most important thing is that you choose an activity you love and are passionate about. Okay, okay. So the word *love* might be pushing it. Even if you find yourself passionately hating it, but you're still doing it, that's great! Find whatever it takes to excite you and motivate you to bounce out of bed in the morning and do your cardio!

While your enjoyment of any chosen activity is important, there are some cardiovascular workouts that are more efficient than others. For example, running, kickboxing, and swimming laps all burn about 300 to 350 calories per half hour, while power walking, hiking, and the use of various cardio machines follow closely with about 200 to 250 calories burned per half hour. You certainly don't have to run or kickbox to get results, but you may want to keep in mind that you will need to walk almost twice as long to get the same fat-burning results as running half the time.

No matter what your fitness level, be assured that walking is an excellent and safe cardiovascular activity choice with plenty of fitness benefits. It still seems to be the all-American favorite participatory form of cardio among women and is preferred over running by almost every chiropractor and physician we know! That's because it is a fun, great way to exercise without putting a lot of strain on your joints and muscles.

If walking is your main activity, be sure to power walk. By power walk we mean drive your arms forward and back and take long, fast-paced strides. None of this lollygagging-around business! Again, if you're pressed for time or if walking bores you, you may want to slowly take up jogging. The only activities we do *not* recommend for maximum fat-burning are golf, tennis, and volleyball. While they are fun, they are stop-and-go sports, which don't always keep you moving for a long enough duration to maximally burn fat. Each of you will begin the Wedding Workout at a different fitness level, and we cannot stress enough the importance of picking an activity that will elevate your heart rate. The table on page 92 will help you to gain perspective on how your active metabolic rate (AMR) is affected by different activities.

Injury Prevention

I personally love to run and kickbox, but I've been most injury prone while doing these activities. Although activities such as running and kickboxing get lots of attention for being the most exciting, energizing, and efficient ways to burn calories, they are high-impact activities that can be tough on your body. The pavement

The Wedding Workout

CALORIES BURNED DURING YOUR FAVORITE ACTIVITIES

	ACTIVITY	CALORIES BURNED	NOTES
	Shopping and registering	126 kcal/hr	Major spree
	Writing invitations, thank-you notes, and more thank-you notes	36 kcal/hr	It never ends . . .
	Running	390 kcal/hr	You go, girl!
	Walking	240 kcal/hr	
	Tennis with the in-laws	207 kcal/hr	Work that forehand!
	Weight training	228 kcal/hr	Lift that diamond!
	Cycling	192 kcal/hr	
	Reading bridal magazines	30 kcal/hr	
	Swimming	270 kcal/hr	Become a bride-to-buoy
	Disco dancing at your bachelorette party	160 kcal/hr	Hello, Mr. Chippendale!

can get really hard after a while! The constant pounding and jumping up and down can lead to injuries such as tendonitis, sprains, strains, bursitis, and stress fractures. These activities are not for everyone. They are for the rigorous athlete or Olympic, die-hard bride who is used to getting in there and going for it! The extra calories burned overexerting yourself are not worth bringing your exercising days to an end. If there is any pain associated with any cardiovascular activity, don't be stubborn and ignore it. Instead, be a smart bride-to-be and be careful! I don't want any of you hobbling down the aisle. If you do feel pain ask yourself, "Is this everyday pain that comes along with exercise, or is it a nagging, sharp, aching pain or burning sensation worthy of my attention?" Anything sharp, nagging, or burning could be an injury. Only you know how much pain you are feeling, and if it is not a good pain, stop! Rest, ice the painful area, if possible elevate it, and if the pain persists, go to see a doctor!

If you prefer something lighter, I recommend low-impact cardiorespiratory activities such as walking, cycling, and swimming. You can also ask the staff at your gym to introduce you to the elliptical training machines such as the Precor. I know the recumbent bike may not seem very intriguing, but it is easy on the knees and allows you to sit back a bit more. You can still work up a good sweat while reading bridal magazines or watching TV. It may be that you have to go a little longer to expend the same number of calories, but be assured the overall fitness benefits are the same.

How Long Should Each Session Last?

On average, I recommend that you do cardio for 20 to 40 minutes; never more, never less. Although you may take a 50- to 60-minute class at your local gym, there is rarely more than 40 minutes of continuous aerobic activity. Regardless of the type of activity you choose, by controlling the duration, frequency, and intensity of the activity, you can effectively use cardiovascular exercise to burn fat and elevate your metabolism. Initially, the length of your cardiorespiratory activity is going to depend on your fitness level; however, in order for you to effectively change your resting metabolic rate (RMR), you must move for a minimum of 20 minutes at a steady pace without stopping. This doesn't mean that if you are running you can't stop to walk. You just need to keep moving. You can burn calories and fat if you move for less than 20 minutes, but you will benefit most by completing 20 continuous minutes of exercise. Therefore, the duration of each session should be a minimum of 20 minutes to a maximum of 40 minutes, depending on which cycle you're in (see table on page 99). If you cannot do 20 minutes, don't get discouraged. Eventually you will be able to and you'll feel great. Just begin by adding one minute per session to whatever you are able to do. No matter how advanced you are, you never need to exceed 40 minutes of cardiorespiratory activity. Don't exercise purge!!! Your health and fitness benefits begin to taper off beyond 40 minutes anyway, and you can actually increase the risk of injury. You want to be a healthy bride, so don't overdo it!

CARDIO CYCLE PROGRESSION RATE

As you progress through the cycles detailed on pages 50–53, the durations and frequencies of your cardio sessions are going to increase. This way each cycle will provide new challenges for the future bride. I don't want any brides getting too comfortable! Don't worry, though! Six weeks at one level will give you all the stamina and confidence you need to take it up a notch. If you are already in good cardiovascular shape when you begin the Wedding Workout, you may already be able to surpass the duration times prescribed for you in each cycle. That's awesome! Congratulations! Hopefully, you will get some tips in the upcoming cross-training section so you can create exciting ways to continually challenge yourself.

If you are new to exercise or you have been inactive for a while, begin cycle 1 nice and easy by power walking at a rapid pace 20 to 25 minutes per cardio session. As soon as you are quite comfortable, increase your intensity and duration. If you're a walker with a secret desire to become a runner, begin integrating 1- to 3-minute runs into your sessions. Keep adding 1 minute each session and you will be running in no time. If you are already in some sort of cardiovascular shape, you can run as long as you are comfortable.

Once you've reached cycle 2, it will definitely be time to step it up. Do so by increasing your cardio session duration to 25 to 30 minutes. By cycle 3, really start to push yourself and take it up to 30 to 35 minutes. Finally, by cycle 4 you will be really ready to challenge yourself by attempting 35 to 40 minutes.

Warm-Up Exercises

When people come late to class, it makes me feel like they are missing out on the most important time of their workout—the warm-up. Warming up is your time to get centered and be present. It is the transition period between time shared with the world and time with yourself. At the beginning and end of each session, regardless of the duration, take 5 minutes to warm up and cool down. Warming up helps you gradually increase your heart rate and body temperature, allowing your muscles to become warmer and more flexible. Also, think of it as a time to get focused, centered, and mentally prepared for your workout. Create a mantra like "I can and will do this." Our favorite warm-ups are walking briskly for 3 to 5 minutes outside or on a treadmill, or doing some high knee marches in place. Always begin and end your cardio sessions with stretching! Even if you are tired and ready to fall into bed, don't forget to stretch! Use the stretches previously mentioned in chapter 4 as your guide. Remember, you want to remain an agile bride and cardio can tighten your muscles, so don't forget to stretch!

HIGH KNEE MARCHES

Ready to march! Begin by standing with your feet firmly planted, hip-width apart and knees slightly bent. Tip your pelvis under and contract your gluteus and abdominal muscles. Inhale and pull your rib cage away from your hips, creating length in your spine. Lift your left knee into your chest as you simultaneously lift your right arm straight up by your right ear. Lower and repeat, lifting your right knee and your left arm. Repeat at least 25 times per side. Really think of pulling your knee to your chest, not your chest to your knee. We love these because right away you can feel a lengthening in your back and arms as you lift opposite hand and foot. It makes an instant connection.

Cross Training

What would your fiancé say if every time you got together you had peanut butter and banana sandwiches? Unless he's Elvis, he probably likes variety and I bet you do, too. An exercise program also needs variety. Enter cross training. By cross training we mean incorporating different types of exercises as well as alternating different training methods into your overall program. The synergistic effect is to balance out muscle groups, create greater strength, enhance leanness, and improve overall workout performance. Our goal is to help you to create variety in your cardio sessions, no matter what your cardiovascular level. Your relationship to fitness is no different than your love relationship. We all know that variety keeps relationships thriving. Likewise, within your weekly car-

Tracy

I believe in the power of cross training. One day I may go at my maximum for 25 minutes and stop. The next day I may work on my endurance and go for a 40-minute early morning run at a nice leisurely pace. Another cardio day may consist of 30 minutes on the Precor machine with a set of minute-long intervals, or a spinning or kickboxing class. One of my favorite things to do is to get outside and run on the UCLA track. I feel so free and empowered! I get completely inspired by the stadium feel and pretend I'm Marion Jones circling the track in Australia at the Olympic games. Scary but true!

dio regimen, not all of your sessions should be the same. If you are one of those people, however, who benefits from the ritual of doing the same thing every time, then we'll allow it and by all means continue. To prevent boredom and workout burnout, we rotate walking, running outside, running on the treadmill, running on the track, biking, swimming, and using the Precor machine at the gym. There are all sorts of ways you can inspire yourself, have fun, and be creative with your cardiovascular exercise. Make it a goal to keep expanding your exercise repertoire. Use your mind as well as your body and your excuse will never be "I'm bored" or "I have a headache."

Time of Day

Not only do I like to vary the speed and duration of my workouts, but I also try to vary the time of day that I exercise. Most people have a time of day when exercise is more effective for them or they are more motivated to do it. Often, I like to exercise first thing in the morning because I get it over with and don't have to worry about fitting it into my schedule later in the day. Not to mention, it really gives me a sense of accomplishment that I carry with me throughout my day. It also helps me to eat healthy foods because I don't want to sabotage the good habits that I've started for the day. Many of my clients find that they perform better at night. They attribute this to the fact that their muscles have been awake all day, and also that they lack the energy in the morning to really go for it. Some even claim that an evening workout helps to relieve their anxieties, reducing insomnia and allowing for more peaceful sleep.

Interval and Endurance Training

Regardless of what activity you choose or the duration of the activity, you are going to be either interval training or endurance training. By endurance training, I mean doing your cardio at a moderate pace for a longer period of time. The goal with endurance training is to increase your aerobic fitness level overall by increasing your stamina or how long you can do an activity without stopping. Ask your fiancé. He'll surely tell you the goal is to go longer. Essentially you'll be able to move for greater periods of time without getting tired, and you will be more fit for your interval training. By interval training, I mean alternating high- and low-intensity levels in measured spurts during a workout. The goal with intervals is to increase your heart rate, then bring it back down again, recover, and increase it again. This type of training allows you to burn more calories in less time, while it also strengthens your heart and lungs.

To include both types of training in your three to five cardiorespiratory sessions, I recommend one general endurance conditioning session, at least one mid-

SAMPLE CARDIO INTERVAL AND ENDURANCE TRAINING CHART

WORKOUT TYPE	DURATION	INTENSITY
General	20–30 minutes	Steady/moderate
Mid-level	25–40 minutes	10–15 minutes at a good pace; rotate 30 seconds at a full stride with 30 seconds recovery; 5-minute cooldown at an easy, moderate pace
Peak	25–40 minutes	Solid push for at least 15 minutes during your workout

level interval session, and one peak-performance session per week. Your peak session can be either an endurance or interval-type session. In your general conditioning session, perform your activity for at least 20 minutes at a nice, comfortable, steady pace. You do not have to kill yourself; rather, go for increasing your endurance and stamina over time. In your mid-level session, try inserting intervals into your workout. Begin at an aerobic pace for 10 to 15 minutes, then rotate 30 seconds on at a nice stride, push, or sprint, followed by 30 seconds off at a much slower recovery pace. Do this for 5 to 10 minutes, followed by 10 more minutes at a steady pace before cooling down. Your peak session per week could also include interval training at a higher intensity or a good push or stride. (See table 5.2.) Whether you are new to exercise or an advanced athlete, you will certainly benefit from mixing up your cardio routine.

Record your progress in the registry in the appendix on page 220. and look at your rate of progression. Keep track of the type of workout you do by using the initials "G," "M," or "P" in the exercise registry. We've included an example of the first column (Cardio) of the exercise registry.

Just remember: If you mix and match activities and intensities, you will always be challenged and will overcome mental and physical plateaus. Perhaps you will want to try a different activity every week during a six-week cycle. For example, you might try running one week, then swimming the next week and cycling the week after. Or, maybe you would like to try cycling all six weeks of a cycle, then follow it with a full cycle of swimming. My favorite approach is to incorporate different activities all week long. This really helps me to stay motivated, and the varied workouts also keep me engaged.

WEEK OF: June 1st	CARDIO
MONDAY	DURATION: 31 min. TYPE: G Ⓜ P ACTIVITY: jog treadmill
TUESDAY	DURATION: TYPE: G M P ACTIVITY: Rest
WEDNESDAY	DURATION: TYPE: Ⓖ M P ACTIVITY: swim
THURSDAY	DURATION: 25 min. TYPE: G M Ⓟ ACTIVITY: Precor
FRIDAY	DURATION: TYPE: G M P ACTIVITY: Rest
SATURDAY	DURATION: 30 min. TYPE: Ⓖ M P ACTIVITY: cycling outdoors
SUNDAY	DURATION: TYPE: G M P ACTIVITY: Rest

Watch the Cardio Fly By

For most of us, cardio sessions can be difficult to do. Sometimes even if you get started, it's even harder to finish. What will make the time go by faster? If you are exercising outside, take the time to enjoy your surroundings, such as the flowers, cool houses, or children playing. Are you stopping to smell the roses, figuratively I mean? Don't really stop to smell the roses. Keep moving! By doing your cardio outside, you can get back to nature and take in the world around you.

Cardio Confidence

Regardless of the activities you choose, remember to include the following in order to get the most out of each cardio session:

- 20 to 40 minutes of continuous movement
- Endurance training
- Interval training
- A variety of activities

Tracy

Tracy's Disco Fever

We've discussed many of the typical cardio activities that brides engage in, but I'm going to let you in on a little secret that I've just rediscovered. Disco dancing came back into my life after a long, slow hike with a client. We turned on '70s disco tunes and what we thought was the end of a session turned into a whole new cardio fantasy come true. We gyrated, jumped, and turned, and most importantly we laughed and had fun. The added bonus was we really sweat and had a great cardio session. Take your newfound inner rhythm and whisk your fiancé off for a romantic evening on the dance floor. It's a great way to burn calories and look hot and sexy while you're doing it. Think of all the great songs you may discover that will help you pick the music for your wedding reception. Add to that the confidence you'll gain to dance on the big day without the help of some stuffy dance instructor. Say good-bye to ballroom dancing and hello to disco dancing! ᶜ

Suzanne

Suzanne's Secret to Cardio Success

I find listening to upbeat music while I do my cardio workout really helps to make the time fly by. I turn up the disco and ride the boogie. Try to think of your workouts as time for yourself. Use that time to visualize your goals, plan your wedding, or fantasize about your fiancé. It is also a great time for making a gratitude list. I compile a mental list and give thanks for all my friends and family who mean so much to me. Doing your cardio with a partner is another surefire way to ease the pain. After all, misery loves company! It is a great way to build a friendship, be an inspiration to someone, or just plain gossip. Do whatever you have to do to let your mind take you away from counting the minutes until your workout is over, and before you know it, it will be. If you are obsessed with the number of minutes, break down the time into 7- to 10-minute increments and the workout will seem more feasible. Here are two tricks that really help me get through my cardio workouts. If I'm on the treadmill for 30 minutes, after the first 15 minutes I pretend that I've just started and then it feels like I'm doing my cardio for only 15 minutes. Trick number two is when I feel like I can't move one more foot and I still have 5 minutes to go, I think of how short a time 5 minutes really is. After all, 5 minutes is a set of commercials during an episode of your favorite sitcom. Then I say to myself, "I can do ANYTHING for 5 minutes!" And you know what? I always manage to do it—and so can you!

Tracy's Cardio Runway

Disco dancing is not the only way you can have fun with cardio. Strut down the cardio fashion highway and head to the mall. You might have to mentally gear up for cardio, but why not literally gear up and go shopping? I suggest that you invest in an outfit or two that you look and feel great in. Remember, it's your time to shop! You're already buying new outfits to look fabulous in for your bridal showers and parties. Why should working out be any different? So, Ms. Bride-to-be, I must ask you: What do you wear when you work out? A baggy T-shirt, baggy pants, or an old '80s Jane Fonda (no offense, Jane!) leotard? Well, you are missing out on all of the awesome workout fashions around that can be one of the fun parts of getting in shape. You don't have to spend a lot of money on fancy exercise outfits. In fact, stores such as Target have great exercise clothes. Go ahead and splurge. Are you ready to put your running shoes on? Do you have a comfortable, snazzy pair you like, or are they the pair you had in gym class fifteen years ago? It may seem funny, but the more I like my shoes and the cooler I feel in them, the more likely I am to use them. To look cool and feel snazzy, I recommend buying a pair of colorful running shoes! When I want to feel strong and motivated, I have been known to wear my bright red Pumas. I promise you, they help me to work harder no matter what kind of mood I'm in. If you don't believe me, just ask some of the students in my class. When they see me walk through the door in my red shoes, they know they are in for a doozy of a session! An attractive outfit can definitely motivate you to perform well and inspire you to "show up" for your workout. Wear clothes that make you feel sexy and attractive. After all, a cool ensemble can help shape up your attitude as well as your figure. ❧

6

The Toned Bride

With cardio you've developed the endurance to withstand wedding planning, and now with musculoskeletal resistance training, the third component of the Wedding Workout, you will build the strength to tackle any obstacle that comes your way. Our hope is that your newfound strength will leave you and your husband fighting over who will carry whom over the threshold.

Can you recall an argument you had with your now-fiancé? While it may have been painful at the time, the argument—the resistance or opposition between the two of you—clearly made your relationship closer and stronger or you would probably not be engaged. Just as resistance in our personal lives and relationships helps us to grow and become stronger, so does musculoskeletal resistance training increase strength in our muscles and bodies overall. Almost every activity we do in life is a form of resistance training. It doesn't matter whether you are getting out of bed, holding yourself in proper posture at the dinner table, or actually lifting a weight; all of these involve musculoskeletal resistance.

As I mentioned before, musculoskeletal resistance training means resistance training with weights and/or performing isometric exercises in order to increase your overall muscle mass, strength, and tone. If you want to lose weight, resistance train- ing combined with cardiorespiratory activity is the most efficient way to go. Cardiorespiratory activity alone helps you to burn calories, but it will not tone your body or create muscle. By combining the two types of training, you will simultane- ously burn fat and create muscle, provided that you are eating well. And remember that since muscle burns more calories than fat, increasing your muscle mass will ele- vate your basal metabolic rate. Musculoskeletal resistance training will help to turn your body into an incinerator, burning fat and calories even when you are at rest! You will look more toned and your stronger muscles will improve your posture.

Whether you're a bride who wants a firmer back, arms, chest, abdominals, lower body, or all of these, musculoskeletal resistance training is for you. It involves detailed toning and shaping exercises that can definitely help you create the bridal body you have always wanted. If you follow the exercises accordingly and do at least two to three resistance-training sessions per week in addition to your cardiorespiratory activity, there is no way you won't get stronger and see results. I promise you there is not a single bride who has not improved when she has done these exercises consistently! Generally, I suggest you rotate your car- diorespiratory days and your resistance-training days. If you want to challenge yourself, or if you've missed a day, it is okay to double up. Just be sure to get one complete day of rest every week.

For each body part, I have included various exercises. I will go over each exercise thoroughly so that you understand exactly what muscles you are working. Additionally, I have included variations to make the exercises easier or more difficult to suit your needs. The level of difficulty for the variations will be indicated by wedding bell icons, with two bells indicating an intermediate level and three bells an advanced level.

If you are a beginner, stay at one wedding bell and use 1- or 2-pound weights. Focus on learning the basics. Proceed slowly and gradually. Give yourself plenty of time to succeed at the single wedding bell level before attempting the more difficult variation. Finally, remember that being a beginner has its advantages—you have nowhere to go but up!

If you already strength train, begin at a level that feels comfortable. Avoid the tendency to rush to the next level. You don't need to prove to yourself that you're in great shape. Don't do too much too fast. Relax and enjoy learning the exercises thoroughly.

Regardless of your fitness level, always be mindful and focused when you are doing resistance training. Do your exercises wholeheartedly and with your undivided attention. Concentrate on feeling your body from the inside out and recognizing your strengths and weaknesses. Don't give way to distractions! Turn off the ringer on your phone if you need to. Stand in front of a mirror so you are constantly aware of your form. Turn on music that inspires and motivates you. Sing out loud if you like! Do whatever you have to do to really make your workout your own. Last but not least, always take a few minutes to sit quietly before and after you work out. Just breathe and sit still for a moment. Think of this as a time for renewal and growth, and the significance of your commitment to the exercises will slowly reveal itself to you.

Your resistance-training session should always include two sets of push-ups as well as at least two exercises per body part. Try to vary the exercises you choose. Also, vary the intensities. That way no two training sessions will be the same, and you won't get bored or reach plateaus. You don't need to do resistance training more than three times a week. Try to train every other day, but if you need to resistance train two days in a row, you can. Just be sure to take a full day of rest after. If you have a specific area, like your stomach, that you really want to work, you can go for it and perform your exercises daily. Just don't overdo it!

THE BUFF BRIDE FEAR FACTOR

Speaking of overdoing it, I know a common concern for brides these days is that they want to get toned, but they are afraid they will bulk up and look like the Incredible Hulk's fiancée. Trust me! The goal here is not to create any buff brides or Mrs. Universe brides. Still, as a woman who has been all different shapes and sizes, I fully understand your fear. So, let's address the buff bride fear factor right now!

After having been a competitive athlete and lifted heavy weights in the gym all my life, I decided I wanted a more sleek, lean, and elongated type of look rather than a bulky one. I stopped lifting heavy weights and starting experimenting with very light weights or no weights at all, instead using my body's own resistance. After trying different classes and exercise techniques, I finally learned how to achieve the elongated, toned appearance I was looking for but that had eluded me. Finally, people no longer asked me if I was a professional speed skater!

I found that by using light weights and very high repetitions for each exercise, I could develop lean muscles without building bulk. Often this means doing lots of repetitions, but by alternating the pace and size of contractions, I never get bored. A set for me usually consists of 8 to 15 long, slow, full-range-of-motion repetitions followed by the same number of shorter, faster, smaller, intense moves or pulses. Finally, the set is completed with a good hold in which my muscles are fully contracted. I call this the long/short training method. I use a high number of fast and slow repetitions to completely fatigue a particular muscle group. This can create a burning sensation—and I love it. Burn, baby, burn! And by mixing the speed and size of your repetitions, you will be maximizing both your slow-twitch and fast-twitch muscle fibers for optimum results!

So far, it has worked for me and for many of the brides I have trained. I've enjoyed my new shape, and I am usually pretty good at maintaining my results. I continue to do the musculoskeletal exercises provided here on a weekly basis. Trust me, these exercises alone will not cause you to bulk up. I do, however, notice that I tend to bulk up a little if I do only my resistance training without incorporating cardiorespiratory activity, along with a healthy diet. Of course, it is a challenge to incorporate all three components all the time! You have to leave room for ebbs and flows, but remember that ultimately it is the combination we are striving for.

GETTING STARTED

For your weight-training exercises, you will need 1- to 5-pound free weights, depending upon your fitness level. You can pick these up at your local sporting goods store. Be sure to pick a color you like! These guys are going to become your friends! I usually use 2-pound weights, and I hardly ever use more than 3 pounds, except for when toning my biceps.

The Pelvic Tilt

For each exercise you will be doing something called the "pelvic tilt" to properly align your body and to help you feel grounded in your center. You may be asking yourself, "What is my center?" As a trainer, my center is my truth, my core, my life force, my center of gravity, my root to the world below me, and finally, my point of connection to myself and to the essence of who I am. In my body, I feel my center in the area just below my belly button and above my genitals. I refer to this area as my pelvic triangle. When I am working out, my pelvic triangle operates as the home base or center from which I initiate any exercise I choose to do. When I focus on tipping my pelvis under and staying centered, I can really feel my body working from the inside out.

While it may seem quite obvious to many of you brides what I mean by your "center," I'd like you to think about how often you actually feel connected to it. (In daily life, most of us go around unaware that we are disconnected from our centers.) In fact, last year I taught a seminar to a group of men and women on body image and on staying centered during workouts. I demonstrated the pelvic tilt and asked everyone to follow me in finding his or her center. One adorable woman broke down in tears because she said she had never felt her center nor did she know how to find it. She had a very difficult time keeping both feet right under her for any length of time. Instead, she resorted to her habitual stance, with one knee very bent and the opposite hip jutting out to the side. Try standing this way and you will see that your back is completely crooked and you have no real grounding force or stability. No wonder the poor thing couldn't find her center!

With this in mind, do not underestimate the power of the pelvic tilt. Regard it as the core of every exercise you do. To find your center, stand relaxed with your head straight up, your chest lifted, and your shoulders back. Your feet should be parallel and hip-width apart, and your knees slightly bent. Take a deep breath and pull all the air up into your chest. As you inhale, pull your rib cage as far away from your hipbones as you can and press your shoulder blades down your back. This creates a wonderful lengthening and energizing sensation in the spine. Then, simultaneously tip your pelvis under, gently squeezing your gluteus, and pull your belly button toward your back. As soon as it feels like your rib cage is actually floating over your hips, you will know you have mastered the pelvic tilt. You will feel centered and ready to go for it!

In this position, you should instantly feel longer, taller, and more energized by the space being created in your whole torso. Maintain this position all the way through each exercise, thereby making your workout a conscious effort to experience yourself and to better get to know who you are. You will be so practiced at feeling centered, you will have no problem feeling grounded and confident as you walk down the aisle!

How Many Sets Should I Do?

It used to be that you were supposed to do three sets of each exercise. I feel, however, that it is much more efficient to do one set of each exercise with enough repetitions to take the muscle to exhaustion. Your point of exhaustion is when you can no longer move without straining the muscle or another body part in order to lift the weight. To get stronger and build muscle, you will want to push the limits of what you are initially able to do, but don't ever push past fatigue! It is unnecessary and has no physiological benefit, and you will only hurt yourself. Regardless of the number of reps prescribed, if you are at fatigue, stop. Never stress or strain. Always listen to your body and let the inner feeling it expresses guide you.

For the isometric exercises, you will use your own body weight to create tension in your muscles. You will perform little pulses combined with holding still while contracting your muscles for a period of time. Owwww! These babies can burn, but they are very effective for creating nice, toned, long-looking muscles. Learn to love the burn! Initially, you may have to take breaks within an exercise. I encourage you to do as much stopping and starting as you need to. Gradually, the goal is to minimize your breaks while increasing your number of repetitions and pulses and the lengths of your holds.

In the following pages I have included all of the exercises you will need to tone your arms and shoulders, back, chest, abdominals, legs, bottom, and thighs. All of these can be performed at the gym or in the privacy of your own home. Keep in mind that unlike your cardio workout, you can accomplish a lot by doing a few sets, even if you only have 10 or 15 minutes available for a workout. Incorporate the stretches from the flexibility section (chapter 4) into the musculoskeletal exercises. As soon as you have worked a body part, stretch it before moving on to the next exercise. Have fun with the musculoskeletal section of the Wedding Workout! Check out our Anatomy Bride so you can be fully aware of which muscles you are working. Isn't she a cutie! Get excited! You are on your way to becoming even more connected to the bride you want to be and to who you truly are! (See page 113.)

ARMS

After going to a number of bridal shops and interviewing numerous brides and seamstresses, we realized that, hands down, every bride cared more about her arms than any other body part. In fact, almost every bride's primary concern with

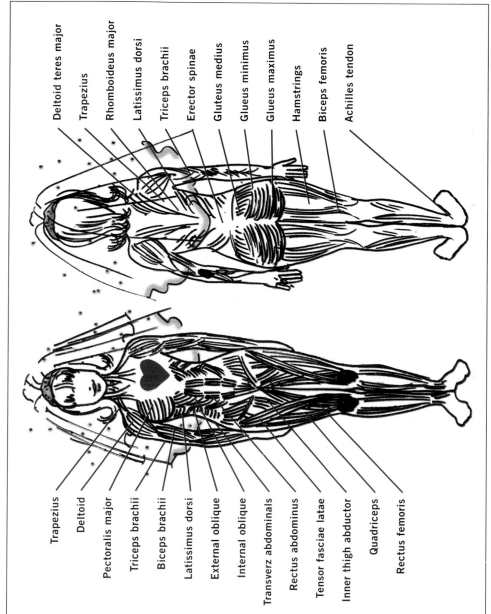

Deltoid teres major
Trapezius
Rhomboideus major
Latissimus dorsi
Triceps brachii
Erector spinae
Gluteus medius
Glueus minimus
Glueus maximus
Hamstrings
Biceps femoris
Achilles tendon

Trapezius
Deltoid
Pectoralis major
Triceps brachii
Biceps brachii
Latissimus dorsi
External oblique
Internal oblique
Transverz abdominals
Rectus abdominus
Tensor fasciae latae
Inner thigh abductor
Quadriceps
Rectus femoris

ANATOMY BRIDE

regard to her dress was, "I want my arms to look good!" It did not seem to matter whether the dress the bride had chosen was sleeveless or long-sleeved. Almost all of the brides had a case of the prewedding arm blues. Many brides complained of having fat, flabby arms whether their arms were oversized or not, and they wanted desperately to know what they could do about it. One bride even held up her arm and began strumming the fleshy underside of her upper arm back and forth, singing "La! La! La!" She had named her "underarm fat" her "La-La's"! The point is that every bride we talked to, no matter the current shape of her arms, wanted to feel confident about her arms on her wedding day. Every bride seems to feel that her arms are being judged as a primary indicator of what kind of shape she is in. And they are right! Toned arms and shoulders, along with good posture, can instantly give you a sense of confidence. With that in mind, I've created the Bride-to-Be Upper-Body Challenge, as well as some other arm-shaping exercises that will get your arms in the shape you want them to be. No matter what style dress you have chosen, your arms and shoulders will command attention!

The Bride-to-Be Upper-Body Challenge includes four styles of push-ups. Two sets will focus on the front of your arms, working your biceps and pectoral muscles more, and two sets will focus on the back of your arms, or triceps muscles. Be sure to do at least one set of push-ups from each muscle group per session. While many brides initially moan and groan when I say it is time for push-ups, they quickly realize that push-ups are a very effective way to hit multiple muscle groups in a short period of time. With push-ups, you can work your pectoral, biceps, triceps, deltoid, rhomboid, and trapezius muscles all at once! Because you don't need any weight or equipment, you can do them anytime and anywhere. Push-ups are one of my favorite ways to tone up and get strong. Once you get used to them, they are very empowering. A little pushing up can go a long way! If you are in a hurry and don't have time for your arm weight work, be sure to get your push-ups in and you will still be in good shape. Push-ups are also a great way to relieve anxiety or nervousness. I sometimes do them before an important meeting or at night when I can't fall asleep. Perhaps you will be doing them in your bridal suite before you walk down the aisle! After you finish your arm and push-up sets, do the Child's Pose (page 74), the Cross-Legged Hip and Tricep Stretch (page 64), and the Wide Leg Downward Dog Stretch (page 76). If you do these stretches immediately following your sets, they will help lengthen the contracted muscles, thereby preventing any bulking potential.

Suzanne

Stretching, while it had been an important part of my exercise program prior to my engagement, became a lifesaver during wedding planning. Often times, stretching on my own and in Tracy's class was one of the only things that helped me to relax, especially as the big day approached. Stretching before and after my workouts not only gave me perspective on what I was about to do but also on what I had just accomplished. The added bonus is that by really concentrating on stretching and increasing my flexibility, my workouts have been more productive and my exercise-related aches and pains have been few and far between. I really do credit stretching as one of the main reasons that I have been able to stay injury free. Regardless of what is on my schedule, I try to begin every morning with various stretches so that I can release tension and start the day off right. ℮

THE BRIDE'S BASIC PUSH-UP

Works biceps, triceps, and pectoral muscles, as well as trapezius and rhomboid muscles; makes you feel strong.

🔔 **Position 1.** Start on your knees. Place your hands flat on the floor in front of you, just a little more than shoulder-width apart. Your fingertips should be facing forward. Keep your back flat, pelvis tipped under, and your abdominals tight. Point your toes and pull your heels in toward your seat.

🔔 **Position 2.** Keeping your body in a straight line, begin to bend your elbows and *slowly* lower your chest toward the floor until your elbows are at a 90-degree angle. Press your palms into the floor. Hold for a full count (1 to 2 seconds) and then *slowly* raise your chest up. Imagine you are pushing a heavy door open and

resist as it closes. Try to stay connected to the movement all the way through. Repeat 8 to 15 times slowly, then follow with 8 to 15 faster repetitions.

🔔🔔 Slowly lower your chest to about 1 inch off the floor, creating an "M" shape with your elbows, chest, and head. Repeat slowly 8 to 15 times, follow with a 3-count hold at the bottom, and then 8 to 15 faster reps.

🔔🔔🔔 After completing your initial slow push-ups, hold your body 1 inch from the floor and do little baby pulses, 1 inch up and 1 inch down for 8 to 15 reps.

Injury Prevention

- Keep your eyes open and your back flat like a plank.
- Keep your pelvis tipped under, with your gluteus and abdominal muscles contracted to support your lower back.
- Keep your neck soft and in alignment with your spine.
- Do not arch your back or push your buns out behind you.
- Do not drop your pelvis below your hips.
- Do not let your shoulders cave in. Only lower yourself as far as you can keep your upper back flat, even it that is just a few inches.
- Move slowly and don't let momentum take over.

THE TONED BRIDE'S STANDING CHAIR PUSH-UP

Works biceps, triceps, and pectoral muscles, as well as trapezius and rhomboid muscles; gives you a beautiful neckline.

△ Position 1. Grasp the back of a sturdy chair (or table or countertop) and walk your feet about 3 feet back. Maintain a flat, straight back and tip your pelvis under, contracting your gluteus and abdominals. Place your feet just a little more than hip-width apart and lift up onto your toes.

△   Position 2. Press your weight into your hands and slowly lower yourself toward the chair at a count of 4. Try to drop your chest or breastbone below your elbows about an inch away from the chair, again trying to create an "M" shape. Once you are down, hold the position for 3 counts before slowly pushing yourself back up. Imagine you are a plank. Keep your whole body tight and taut. Repeat 8 to 15 times.

🔔🔔 After your final slow repetition, hold your body about an inch away from the chair and pulse your body in tiny movements: 1 inch up and 1 inch down. Repeat 8 to 15 times before pushing back up.

🔔🔔🔔 Perform the initial set, only this time place your hands directly under your shoulders. Remember your plank position and as you lower yourself, keep your elbows directly by your sides. Do not let them move away from your body. Repeat 4 to 8 times. These are difficult, so don't feel bad if you can only do a few.

Injury Prevention
- Keep your eyes open and your back flat like a plank.
- Keep your pelvis tipped under, with your gluteus and abdominal muscles contracted to support your lower back.
- Keep your neck soft and in alignment with your spine.
- Do not arch your back or push your buns out behind you.
- Do not drop your pelvis below your hips.
- Do not let your shoulders cave in. Only lower yourself as far as you can keep your upper back flat.
- Move slowly and don't let momentum take over.

THE BRIDE'S UNDERARM-TIGHTENING TRICEPS PUSH-UP

Tones the triceps muscles and works the "La-La's," also known to many brides as the under-the-arm wedding dress jiggles. "La-La's" be gone!

⚘ Position 1. Sit on the floor. Place your hands behind you and your feet flat on the floor in front of you, making a "table" out of your body. Lift your hips and bend your knees. Keep your shoulders and your body weight directly over your hands. Tip your chin up slightly toward the ceiling. This will help keep your shoulders directly over your hands to target your triceps more.

⚘ Position 2. Bend your elbows, keeping them aimed straight back as if a rubber band was wrapped around them, holding them in place. Slowly lower your body toward the floor. Try to reach at least a 90-degree angle with your elbows before pressing back up to the top. Imagine lifting yourself backward out of a swimming pool. Repeat 8 to 15 times, deep and slow, then follow with 8 to 15 baby pulses.

🔔🔔 Repeat the initial series, only this time start on your heels as opposed to flat-footed. Also, when you perform your little pulses, cross one foot over the opposite knee for 8 reps, then switch sides.

🔔🔔🔔 Triceps Push and Kick: Repeat the first set, but as you press back up, simultaneously kick one leg straight up. Return the foot to the floor as you bend elbows again, then kick up the other leg as you press back up. Repeat 8 to 15 times per side.

Injury Prevention

- Keep your eyes open and either look straight ahead or slightly tip your chin up toward the ceiling.
- Be careful not to let your elbows flail out to the sides.
- Keep your shoulders directly over your hands and do not let your body weight shift out in front of you.
- Place a towel or pillow under your hands if you find there is too much pressure on your wrists.
- Be sure you are bending your elbows and that you are not just swinging your midsection up and down.

THE STRONG BRIDE'S ONE-ARM PUSH-UP

Tones your triceps, biceps, and pectoral muscles. Who says Madonna's got anything on you?

△ Position 1. Sit on your left bottom with your legs together, knees bent, and feet to your right. Lean to your left and as you do, place your right palm on the floor directly in front of your right chest, directly underneath your right shoulder and clear of your legs. Cross your left arm underneath your right arm and clasp your left hand to your right back and rib cage.

△ Position 2. Inhale and press your right palm into the floor. Slowly lower the left side of your head (not your shoulder) to the floor. When your elbow is bent 90 degrees and your head is barely touching the floor, let your body weight drop, press your palm firmly against the floor, and exhale slowly as you push yourself back up. Repeat slowly 8 to 15 times, then switch sides. Try to go very slowly and feel each part of the movement.

🔔🔔 Repeat slowly 8 to 15 times, then follow with 8 to 15 fast repetitions.

🔔🔔🔔 After you have completed your slow repetitions, hold yourself with your elbow bent at 90 degrees. Press into the floor for 5 seconds without moving, then press 1 inch up and 1 inch down quickly for 8 to 15 repetitions.

Injury Prevention

- Keep your eyes open so you don't hit your head on the floor.
- Move slowly, using the floor for resistance at all times.
- Remember that you are moving your body, it's not moving you. Don't allow momentum to take over.

OVERALL ARM AND SHOULDER TONERS

THE BASIC BRIDAL BICEPS CURL

Works the biceps and gives you quick confidence.

🔔   Position 1. Stand with your feet firmly planted, hip-width apart and knees slightly bent. Tip your pelvis under and contract your gluteus and abdominal muscles. Inhale and pull your rib cage away from your hips, creating length in your spine. With a weight in each hand, place your elbows by your sides at hip level. Turn your hands palms forward.

🔔   Position 2. Exhale and slowly curl the weights up to shoulder level. Hold and contract the muscles, then lower the weights back down to the starting position. Repeat 8 to 15 times.

🔔🔔 Once you've completed your reps, bring your arms to a 90-degree angle at your elbows and hold for 3 counts while contracting the muscles. Then bring the weights to your shoulders and hold for 3 counts. Return again to 90 degrees for your final 3-count hold before lowering the weights and repeating the sequence. Focus on a full deep squeeze with each hold. Repeat 8 to 15 times.

🔔🔔🔔 Raise your elbows to shoulder height in front of you and hold your fists directly over your elbows. Perform biceps curls by straightening your arms out parallel to the floor and then curling them back toward your shoulders in one fluid motion. Repeat 8 to 15 times.

Injury Prevention

- Keep your eyes straight ahead.
- Relax your neck and shoulders at all times.
- Avoid leaning back.
- Don't swing the weight or use momentum.

OUT-IN-AND-UP (Simple Variation)

Works biceps, triceps, and deltoids. This one takes a little more concentration, but your new toned arms will be worth it.

🔔 Position 1. Stand with your feet firmly planted, hip-width apart and knees slightly bent, and tip your pelvis under. Inhale and pull your rib cage away from your hips, creating length in your spine. With a weight in each hand, bring your elbows up to shoulder height in front of you. Each elbow should be straight in front of each shoulder. Position your fists directly over your elbows with your palms turned toward you.

🔔 Position 2. Keeping your biceps tight, slowly lift your elbows 1 inch up and then drop 1 inch down. Repeat 8 to 15 times.

🔔🔔 Following your slow contractions, pulse up and down 8 to 15 times.

OUT-IN-AND-UP (Advanced Variation)

🔔 Position 1. Stand with your feet firmly planted, hip-width apart and knees slightly bent. Tip your pelvis under and contract your gluteus and abdominal muscles. Inhale and pull your rib cage away from your hips, creating length in your spine. With a weight in each hand, raise your elbows to shoulder height in front of you. Hold your fists directly over your elbows, with your palms turned toward you.

🔔 Position 2. Inhale and contract your biceps muscles. Slowly extend the weights OUT in front of you until your arms are straight. Continue contracting your biceps and slowly curl the weights back IN to your starting position. Slowly lift your elbows 1 inch UP and then drop them 1 inch down before doing the entire sequence over again. Repeat 8 to 15 times.

🔔🔔 Before you begin to extend your arms out, simply lift and lower your elbows, 1 inch up and 1 inch down, pulsing at least 15 times before you begin the *out-in-and-up* sequence.

🔔🔔🔔 Perform the entire sequence 8 times slowly, then 8 times quickly. Finish with 8 small pulses, moving your elbow up and down 1 inch. Finally, hold the weights in the *up* position for 5 seconds and then stop.

🔔🔔🔔 Finally, press your elbows and forearms together with palms facing each other and continue pulsing up and down in small, controlled, fast movements. Pulse 8 to 15 times.

Injury Prevention

- Keep your eyes straight ahead and your head up.
- Keep your neck and shoulders relaxed at all times.
- Move slowly until you get the rhythm of the motion.

TRICEPS TONER

Works the triceps in a major way. Think small, intense, powerful moves, and *voilà!* Say hello to your triceps!

🔔 Position 1. Hold a weight in each hand and set your right leg in front of you in a lunge position. If you are familiar with yoga, think of the warrior pose. Be sure to keep your back straight and your shoulders square. Rest your right hand on your right knee and maintain a straight, tight back leg. Extend your left arm straight out behind you at shoulder level and hold it. Hold the weight in a vertical position with your palm facing your side or rib cage.

⌂ Position 2. Exhale and bring your arm in toward your rib cage. Hold it there 1 second. Then, squeeze the back of your arm and lift your arm at least ½ inch toward the ceiling. Hold there 1 second and then repeat from the beginning 8 to 15 times. Imagine you are squeezing a ball between your arm and your rib cage on the "in" part of the exercise, and that you are pressing your arm against the ceiling on the "up" part of the exercise. Think "isolation." Do a full set on one side, then switch and repeat on the other side.

⌂⌂ After you have completed your in-up-hold repetitions, continue to hold the straight arm behind you and begin to move the weight up and down in tiny pulses. At the top of each pulse, pause for 1 to 2 seconds. Repeat 8 to 15 times. Think of squeezing on the "up" part of the exercise.

⌂⌂⌂ After both sets of repetitions, bend and straighten your arm in a kickback motion 8 to 15 times.

Injury Prevention

- Keep your eyes looking down at the floor and your head and neck soft.
- Do not bounce the weight in and up.
- Keep your shoulders square and equal distance from the floor. Don't let your working-arm shoulder roll back.

LIFT THE BUCKET TRICEPS TONER

Works the triceps and biceps and makes you feel powerful. You'll definitely be able to lift your own honeymoon luggage.

🔔   Position 1. Stand with your feet firmly planted, hip-width apart and knees slightly bent. Tip your pelvis under and contract your gluteus and abdominal muscles. With a weight in each hand and your palms facing forward, position your arms by your sides. If it feels more comfortable, you can place one foot forward.

🔔   Position 2: Exhale and slide your elbows up behind your rib cage. Imagine that you're pulling up a weighted bucket behind you with each hand. Lift your elbows to the highest point you can without tightening your neck and lifting your shoulders. Slowly lower your elbows to the starting position. Repeat 8 to 15 times.

🔔🔔 Hold your last repetition at the highest point and do small pulses up and down. Repeat 8 to 15 times.

🔔🔔🔔 After completing your initial repetitions, hold your elbows at the top, pulse up twice, and then extend your arms straight back in a kickback motion as you tighten your triceps. Repeat 8 to 15 times.

Injury Prevention

- Keep your eyes straight ahead.
- Make sure that your shoulders stay down and relaxed.
- Avoid rounding your back if you lean forward.

STARTING BLOCK TRICEPS KICKBACK

Works the triceps, biceps, quadriceps, and gluteus muscles and makes you feel like a real athlete. Ready, set, go!

🔔   Position 1. Crouch down with your right foot in front of you. Place both hands on the floor in front of you as though you are at the starting line of a 100-yard dash. Your left knee should be on the floor with your right knee near your right shoulder. You should have a weight under your left hand. Lift your hips until you are in the "get set" position.

🔔   Position 2: Extend your left arm straight back. Bend your knees halfway down as you simultaneously curl the weight in (biceps). Lift your hips up again, straightening the knees as you extend your left arm back (triceps).

Repeat 20 to 30 times, then change sides. You can vary the speed at which you perform the exercise.

Injury Prevention

- Keep your eyes focused on the floor in front of you.
- Keep your neck and shoulders relaxed.
- If you feel any pain in your knees, stop immediately.
- Move slowly until you get the rhythm of the motion.

THE SQUEEZE

Works the deltoids, pectorals, trapezius and rhomboid muscles, and triceps. This one just feels good. It's not called "the squeeze" for nothing.

🔔 Position 1. Stand with your feet firmly planted, hip-width apart and knees slightly bent. Tip your pelvis under and contract your gluteus and abdominal muscles. Inhale and pull your rib cage away from your hips, creating length in your spine. With a weight in each hand, turn your palms down and extend your arms in front of you at chest level. Bring your arms together so the heads of the weights are touching.

🔔 Position 2. Exhale and slowly move your arms to your sides at shoulder height. Once your arms are directly out to each side, slowly begin to rotate your fists downward and your palms up to the ceiling as you bring your arms

all the way behind your back. Try to get the heads of the weights to touch behind you as well. Then return your arms to the front, rotating your fists and palms back up as you go. Imagine there is an air bag in front of you and behind you. Try to squeeze all the air out as you bring the weights together both in front and behind. Repeat 8 to 15 times slowly, then follow with 8 to 15 fast repetitions.

🔔🔔 After your repetitions, keep your hands in front of you with your palms down and cross the heads of the weights over and under each other 50 or more times. This will tighten your chest just below your underarms and prevent the appearance of "bridal underarm chest fat."

🔔🔔🔔 Bring your arms behind your back and with your palms up continue to pulse the heads of the weights together for a count of 50. Focus on squeezing the backs of the arms, or triceps muscles.

Injury Prevention

- Keep your eyes open and look straight ahead.
- Keep your shoulders and neck relaxed and your head upright.
- Don't swing the weights; rather, use slow, controlled movements.
- Try to keep your arms as straight as possible.

SHOULDER TONER

Works the anterior, medial, and posterior deltoids. This one will guarantee your shoulders look great in any bridal gown.

🔔 Position 1. Stand with your feet firmly planted, hip-width apart and knees slightly bent. With a weight in each hand, face your palms downward and rest your hands on your quadriceps. Tip your pelvis under and contract your gluteus

and abdominal muscles. Inhale and pull your rib cage away from your hips, creating length in your spine.

🔔 Position 2. Exhale and lift both arms in front of you until they are slightly above shoulder height. Lower both arms without dropping the weight to a point of no resis-

tance. Lift the weights out to the sides until they are slightly above shoulder level. Your fists should be rotated downward. Pause briefly and then lower your arms again. Repeat 8 to 15 times.

🔔🔔 After your initial slow repetitions, immediately do 8 to 15 at a faster pace.

🔔🔔🔔 After your last repetition to the sides, hold your arms still at shoulder height. Turn your fists slightly downward with palms facing behind you. Pulse your arms up and down 8 to 15 times. Then hold for 5 seconds before returning your arms to your sides.

Injury Prevention
- Keep your eyes open and focus straight ahead.
- Avoid leaning back, and keep your upper body still.
- Keep your arms straight, but do not lock them at the elbow.
- Do not swing the weights or use momentum to lift them.

BACK

While arms may be the number one body part brides-to-be moan about, backs surely follow a close second. Think about it. Your walk down the aisle will take only a minute or two, but you'll be standing in front of family and friends with your back to them for at least a good half hour. If you're having a religious ceremony, you might be up there as long as an hour—but by then your guests probably won't be looking at your back but the back of their eyelids. Seriously, though, your back is going to get a lot of time in the spotlight, and a defined back is a beautiful thing. Some dresses have more back coverage than others, but if you will be showing some skin, you may want to really concentrate on the back exercises in the Wedding Workout.

Finally, a strong back is essential for maintaining a healthy physique as well as good posture, and it will assist you greatly when training other body parts. Follow your back exercises with the Ball Stretch (page 67) and Ball Stretch Number Two (page 68). The Cobra (page 72) and the Camel (page 73) are also excellent for stretching out your spine and back.

THE OPEN-BACK WEDDING DRESS TONER

Works the erector spinae, rhomboids, and posterior deltoids, and by crunch time this one will help ease the weight of wedding planning on your back.

Position 1. Stand with your feet firmly planted, hip-width apart and knees slightly bent. Tip your pelvis under and pull your abdominals in. With a weight in each hand, place your arms straight out in front of you at shoulder height with your palms turned downward.

🔔 Position 2. Inhale and pull your elbows straight back while squeezing your shoulder blades together. You will most likely not touch your elbows together, but try. Repeat 8 to 15 times.

🔔🔔 Follow your initial repetitions with 8 to 15 tiny pulses, keeping your elbows at their furthest point back before returning them to the front.

🔔🔔🔔 Repeat the entire sequence with heavier weights or try repeating the entire sequence two more times.

Injury Prevention

- Keep your eyes straight ahead.
- Keep your shoulders relaxed.
- Move slowly and do not swing the weights back and forth.
- If you need more back support, stand with your back pressed against a doorjamb and your feet just hip-width apart. Slide down the doorjamb. Try to squeeze the doorjamb with your elbows.

THE "T" BACK EXTENSION

Works the rhomboids and erector spinae, and gives you a sexy, toned, elegant back fit for any rehearsal dinner dress.

⌂ Position 1. Lie facedown on the floor with a weight in each hand and your arms extended out from your shoulders. Tip your pelvis into the floor and contract your gluteus and abdominal muscles.

⌂ Position 2. Inhale, then exhale as you slowly raise your chest off the floor. Simultaneously raise your arms, forming a "T" while contracting your back muscles. Hold 1 count, then gently lower yourself back to the floor. Repeat 8 to 15 times.

🔔🔔 After your last repetition, hold your contraction and pulse your arms up and down 8 to 15 times before returning them to the floor.

🔔🔔🔔 Complete with a final hold for 15 to 30 seconds. You can also try forming "A's"—arms out front—and "I's"—arms by your sides—for variation.

Injury Prevention

- Keep your eyes straight ahead.
- Move slowly and do not jerk upward.
- Do not arch your neck back. Keep your neck soft.

OVER-THE-HEAD BACK AND LAT PULLDOWN

Works the latissimus dorsi, trapezius, and rhomboids. This is an all-over back bonus.

🔔 Position 1. Stand with your feet firmly planted, hip-width apart and knees slightly bent. Tip your pelvis under and contract your gluteus and abdominal muscles. Inhale and pull your rib cage away from your hips, creating length in your spine. Hold a weight in each hand with your arms at your sides.

🔔 Position 2. Raise your arms above and a little in front of your head, bringing the heads of the weights together. Exhale and lower your elbows behind your rib cage. Imagine you have a balloon under each arm and your goal is to pop the balloons. Squeeeeeze! Pause, inhale, and bring your arms back overhead. Repeat 8 to 15 times.

△△ After completing the initial repetitions, follow with 8 to 15 faster repetitions.

Injury Prevention

- Keep your eyes straight ahead.
- Make sure you lower the weights parallel with our sides, not behind your neck and head.
- Keep your chest lifted.
- Keep your neck and shoulders relaxed.

CHEST

You may think everyone will be staring at your arms jiggling as you walk down the aisle. The truth is that whether you're a B cup, a D cup, or a nonexistent cup, your chest and the way you hold yourself are a major focus during the wedding procession. All brides-to-be are conscious of that when choosing a dress. That's why choosing the right neckline to flatter your chest is so important. While the neckline is key, the Wedding Workout chest exercises will only enhance your whole upper body. Following your chest exercises, do the Cobra (page 72), the Camel (page 73), Child's Pose (page 74), or Ball Stretch (page 67).

THE OPEN–CLOSE CHEST ENHANCER

Works the pectoral muscles and biceps, and firms your bust.

△ Position 1. Stand with your feet firmly planted, hip-width apart and knees slightly bent, with a weight in each hand and your palms facing inward. Tip your pelvis under and contract your gluteus and abdominal muscles. Inhale and pull your rib cage away from your hips, creating length in your spine. Lift both arms out to the sides at shoulder height. Bend your arms to form a right angle with each elbow. You will look something like a football stadium goalpost.

△ Position 2. Exhale and begin to contract your chest as you bring your forearms together, hopefully until they touch. Lead with your elbows, not with your fists. Pretend there is an air bag between your arms and you squeeze all the air out! Return to the beginning position and repeat 8 to 15 times.

🔔🔔 Following your initial repetitions, repeat 8 to 15 times at a faster pace.

🔔🔔🔔 Finish by tapping your elbows together, while squeezing and contracting your chest with each tap. Repeat 8 to 15 times.

Injury Prevention

- Keep your eyes straight ahead and your neck and shoulders relaxed.
- Avoid leaning back.
- Keep your arms straight up and your elbows at 90 degrees.
- Keep your elbows at chest level.

THE CLAM

Works the pectoral muscles and firms your breasts. Good-bye, Wonderbra!

🔔 Position 1. Stand with your feet firmly planted, hip-width apart and knees slightly bent, with a weight in each hand and your palms facing inward. Tip your pelvis under and contract your gluteus and abdominal muscles. Inhale and pull your rib cage away from your hips, creating length in your spine. Lift both arms out to the sides at shoulder height, and form a right angle with each elbow as in the previous exercise. This time, though, bring your weights and hands together. Interlace your fingers in a tight grip around the weights while pushing your elbows to the sides, thus creating a triangle.

⌂   Position 2. Imagine a clam opening and closing, and slowly squeeze your elbows together until they touch. Hold the squeeze, then slowly open to the original triangle position. Repeat 8 to 15 times.

⌂⌂   Following your initial repetitions, do 8 to 15 small, 1-inch pulses, tapping your elbows together.

Injury Prevention

- Keep your eyes focused on your fists.
- Keep your elbows in front of your shoulders.
- Keep your neck and shoulders relaxed.

THE CROSSOVER CHEST SQUEEZE

Works the pectorals, deltoids, and biceps; yet another great chest enhancer. And it's fun, too!

🔔 **Position 1.** Stand with your feet firmly planted, hip-width apart and knees slightly bent, with a weight in each hand and your palms facing inward. Tip your pelvis under and contract your gluteus and abdominal muscles. Inhale and pull your rib cage away from your hips, creating length in your spine. Lift both arms out to the sides at shoulder height and form a right angle with each elbow. Remember the goalpost? It's the same thing here.

🔔 **Position 2.** Keeping your biceps tight, squeeze your chest and cross one elbow directly over the other, alternating 8 to 15 times per side. Try to keep your arms completely vertical all the way through.

🔔🔔 Following your initial repetitions, do 8 to 15 small crosses, barely moving your elbows away from each other before crossing them. Keep the tension going, as though you are holding something against your chest and can't let it drop to the floor.

Injury Prevention

- Keep your eyes focused on your fists.
- Make sure you cross your elbows and not your wrists.
- Keep your elbows in front of your shoulders.
- Keep your neck and shoulders relaxed.

STOMACH

Unless you will be wearing a baby doll dress as your wedding dress, your stomach will show in some way through your gown. If you work your upper abdominals, when you step into that bathing suit on your honeymoon we guarantee your tight midsection will get rave reviews from your husband and you'll feel like a million bucks. Even though your stomach will be garnering the same attention as your arms, back, and stomach on your wedding day, it is a major problem area for women. Everybody wants a flat stomach, but remember that your stomach also has a very important job. It is your center, the strength that holds your entire body together. Not to mention, strong abdominal muscles help to support a strong back, which in turn will help you to hold your head up high and your shoulders back as you walk down the aisle. Generally, stomach muscles recover from exercise very quickly. If you are dying for some tight abs, go ahead and do your abdominal exercises every day. After completing your abdominal sets, do the Cobra (page 72), the Camel (page 73), or the advanced version of the Camel (page 73).

FLAT TUMMY TONER

Works rectus abdominus and transverse abdominus and helps to pull in your abs below the belly button, which is a hard area to hit.

🔔   Position 1. Lie flat on your back with your hands by your sides and your right foot crossed over your left at the ankle. Lace your fingers behind your head. Tip your pelvis under, contracting your gluteus and pulling your lower back into the floor. The goal is to create a slight "C" shape through your midsection.

🔔   Position 2. Keeping your back flat, attempt to lift your shoulder blades off the floor as high as you can. Imagine a string pulling your shoulders toward the ceiling. At the top of the contraction, hold for 1 to 2 seconds, or challenge your-self and hold for 5 seconds, before

returning your shoulder blades to the floor. Repeat 25 times. Then, cross your left foot over your right ankle and repeat 25 more times.

🔔🔔 After your initial repetitions, hold at your highest point of contraction and do ¼-inch pulses. Repeat the pulses 25 times per side.

🔔🔔🔔 Take your right arm behind your right ear and twist your palm away from your head. Do the same with your left arm and interlock your fingers, using your extended arms to cradle your head. Press your biceps to your ears and curl your interlaced hands and shoulders up toward the ceiling. Repeat 25 times.

Injury Prevention

- Keep your eyes focused on the ceiling.
- Don't let your abdominals pop out.
- Lift from your abdominals, not from your neck.
- Don't arch your back.

ABDOMINAL STAIRCLIMBER

Works the transverse abdominus quickly and intensely. This is great for your lower abdominals and any drop-waist or sheath-style dress.

🔔 Position 1. Lie on your back with both legs straight up in the air. Lace your fingers behind your head with your elbows to the sides.

🔔 Position 2. Pull your right knee in toward your chest, contracting your lower abdominals. At the same time, pull your left bottom up off the floor as you push your straight left leg toward the ceiling. Repeat the motion on the left side and continue side to side in a reverse climbing motion. Repeat 20 times per side. If your seat doesn't come off the floor at first, that's okay.

🔔🔔 Repeat by alternating slow repetitions with fast ones in sets of 10.

Injury Prevention

- Keep your eyes focused on the ceiling.
- Keep your legs pointed straight up to the ceiling.
- Lift from your abdominals, not from your neck.

ABDOMINAL CURL-IN

Works rectus abdominus and transverse abdominus, and again is great for isolating the lower abdominals.

⛀ Position 1. Lie partially on your back with your elbows on the floor behind you supporting your upper body off the floor. Place your right foot on your left knee and lift your left leg about 2 inches off the floor. Your legs should make the shape of the number 4. Tip your pelvis under, contract your lower abdominals, and hold.

⛀ Position 2. Slowly curl your right knee in toward your chest while continuing to balance your right foot on your left knee. Slowly lower your legs and hold for a 4-count before repeating. Repeat 8 to 15 times per side.

⛀⛀ Following your initial repetitions, hold your legs halfway between the floor and your chest. Pulse your knee toward your chest 8 to 15 times. Switch sides and repeat.

⛀⛀⛀ In the starting position, hold one leg straight out while pulling the other toward your chest as if you were riding a recumbent bicycle. Alternate and repeat 8 to 15 times per side.

Injury Prevention

- Keep your eyes focused on your knees.
- Keep your pelvis tipped under and your stomach pulled in at all times.
- If your lower back begins to hurt, discontinue this exercise.

OBLIQUE TUMMY TONER

Works the internal and external obliques. These concentrated moves will help you look great in any honeymoon bikini.

Position 1. Lie flat on your back with your knees bent and feet hip-distance apart. Tip your pelvis under and press your lower back into the floor. Place both hands under your right knee and lift your elbows to the sides. Imagine creating a "C" shape through your arms and torso. Try to look like the bottom of a ladle or an ice cream scoop. Think of scooping out your insides to get as round as you can.

△ Position 2. With your chin down and your back slightly rounded, curl your chest straight up toward your right knee. This is a small, intensive motion. Hold at your highest point for 2 counts before lowering your chest. Repeat 8 to 15 times per side.

△△ After completing your initial repetitions, extend your right arm straight and hold up your hand in a "stop" position. Place your left palm over your right hand and pulse 8 to 15 times per side.

Injury Prevention

- Keep your eyes focused on your thighs.
- Keep your chin down.
- Keep your neck and shoulders relaxed. Your neck may feel tense the first few times. Take a deep breath to help relax the neck. Also, you can put one hand behind your head if this helps. Be sure to lift from your stomach, not your neck. This tension will diminish as you get stronger.

OBLIQUE TUMMY TONER NUMBER TWO

Works internal and external obliques, and helps get you that toned tummy you've always dreamed of.

🔔 Position 1. Lie on your left side with your knees bent and your feet crossed at the ankle. Extend your right arm out straight behind your right hip. Place your left hand behind your head. Tip your pelvis under and contract your abdominals.

🔔 Position 2. Attempt to pull your left shoulder off the floor as high as possible. Lower your upper body to the floor. Repeat 8 to 15 times on each side.

🔔🔔 After the initial repetitions, hold your upper body at the highest point and pulse 8 to 15 times per side. Try not to let your shoulder touch the floor.

Injury Prevention

- Keep your eyes focused on one point: either choose an object straight ahead or focus on the fingertips of your extended arm.
- Don't lift from your neck.

WAIST

Take a look at the names of the different wedding dress styles: princess waist, basque waist, empire waist. Hopefully, we've just made our point, but in case we haven't, a bride-to-be should never underestimate the role of her waist in her wedding dress. A bride's waist is a critical factor in how her dress will fall. Some dress styles create a slimming look, but if you want to streamline your waist even further, the following exercises will definitely do the trick. Work on creating the love without the handles. Following your waist workout, do the Steeple Side Stretch (page 77) and the Deep Side Stretch (page 71).

WHITTLE YOUR WAIST

Works the external and internal obliques and waistline, as well as the lower back. This exercise will make you feel long and stretched throughout your midsection.

🔔 Position I. Hold a weight on each hip, palms facing inward. Stand with your feet wide apart, your knees bent, and your toes slightly turned out. Tip your pelvis under and contract your gluteus and abdominal muscles. Inhale and pull your rib cage away from your hips, creating length in your spine. Keep your shoulders back, your chest up, and your torso directly over your hips and not in front of your knees.

🔔 Position 2. Don't move from the waist down. Exhale and reach with your right hand straight down your side toward your right ankle. As you reach, your left hand should slide up the left side of your body toward your armpit. Create as much length as you can between your left hipbone and your right fingertips. Really try to touch your ankle. Reach, hold, and then return to the center. Pause for 1 count, inhale, exhale, and then repeat on your left side. Repeat 15 times per side.

🔔🔔 For more intensity, go from side to side without pausing in the center. Repeat 25 times per side.

🔔🔔🔔 Finally, after going side to side, stay to one side and pulse to each ankle 25 times. Careful, this one can make you sore!!! Take time to build up reps, pace, and intensity.

Injury Prevention

- Keep your eyes open and look straight ahead to avoid getting dizzy.
- Take time to warm up the lower back and sides by going slow and steady at first.
- Keep your head up and your shoulders right over your hips, not out in front of them.
- Keep your pelvis tipped under and your bottom and abdominal muscles contracted to support your lower back.

WHITTLE YOUR WAIST, THE SEQUEL

Also works external and internal obliques, and makes your feel taller, leaner, and longer.

🔔 Position 1. Stand with your feet together and your left palm pressed against a wall. Using the wall for stability, and with your body weight on your right foot, turn your right foot away from the wall, point your toe, and slide your right foot directly out to the side. Raise your right arm up to your left ear.

🔔 Position 2. Use your pelvic tilt and squeeze your gluteus. Inhale, exhale, and simultaneously bring your left knee and left elbow together. Hold for 1 count. Then return your left toe to the floor while you reach your left arm back up over your head. When you extend out, imagine reaching toward the highest place on the wall you can with your fingertips.

When you squeeze the knee and elbow together, imagine breaking an egg with your waist. Repeat 25 times per side.

🔔🔔 Pick up your pace and increase your repetitions to 40 per side.

🔔🔔🔔 Increase your repetitions to 50 per side, varying the pace.

Injury Prevention

- Use your arm and press into the wall for stability.
- Keep your eyes fixed on one point out in front of you.
- Keep your pelvis tipped under and your bottom squeezed to prevent your hip flexors from doing all the work.
- Keep your head still and your shoulders back. Move slowly and steadily until you feel warmed up.

WAIST TWISTER

Works the external and internal obliques, while creating an energizing sensation throughout your body.

🔔 Position 1. Spread your feet wide so that they are more than shoulder-width apart. Bend your knees and tip your pelvis under. Bring your arms up to shoulder height and bend your elbows to make right angles, again like a field goal.

🔔 Position 2. Begin rotating side to side from the waist up. Imagine you are a sprinkler. As you rotate, look back over each shoulder and try to move your arm as far behind your back as you can. Repeat 25 to 50 times per side.

Injury Prevention

- Move slowly at first until you feel warmed up.
- Keep your eyes focused on your fingertips.
- Keep your lower body still.

LOWER BODY

Not only will your back be in the spotlight during your ceremony, but it will be sharing the stage with your gluteus maximus, otherwise known as your "booty." I don't know too many women who list their rear as a favorite body part. And let's not forget about your legs, thighs, hips, and calves, which may not be in the spotlight when you're dressed in your wedding gown but will certainly be front and center during your honeymoon! These exercises will help tone, tighten, and lift your bottom and pull in the sides. That's all a girl over sixteen could ask for. After completing your lower-body workout, do any of the following stretches: Inner-Thigh Stretch (page 63), Deep Quad Stretch (page 65), Opposite Hand to Foot Stretch (page 66), Straight Leg Stretch (page 69), Forward Bend Stretch (page 75), and Standing Quadriceps Stretch (page 78).

WALL SIT AND PUNCH

Works the quadriceps and gluteus maximus, as well as your arms. Want to tighten the skin on your legs? Have a wall sit. Improving your musculature provides a better support structure and improves the appearance of your skin.

⌂ Position 1. Stand flat against a wall. Keep your shoulders and back against the wall and walk your feet 1½ feet in front of you. Slide down the wall until you are sitting with your thighs parallel to the floor and your knees bent at a 90-degree angle. Keep your ankles directly under your knees.

🔔 Position 2. Hold this position and alternate punching your fists forward for at least 50 counts (with or without weights).

🔔🔔 Repeat and try 100 punches. This exercise should leave your legs shaking.

Injury Prevention

- Keep your eyes focused straight ahead.
- Keep your back and shoulders flat against the wall.
- Keep your head up.
- Keep your ankles under your knees.

WALL PLIÉ

Works the gluteus maximus, medius, and minimus. This one is also great for toning your hips, thighs, and calves.

🔔 Position 1. Stand with your back against a wall, your feet more than shoulder-width apart, and your toes turned out. Place your hands on your thighs and slowly slide your back down the wall until your thighs are parallel to the floor. You can also do this one by holding on to a sturdy chair placed in front for support.

🔔 Position 2. Hold the plié and pulse up and down 1 inch for 50 repetitions.

🔔🔔 After initial repetitions, rise up on your toes for 2 counts and lower for 2 counts to work your calves. Repeat 8 to 15 times.

🔔🔔🔔 Finally, slowly press your knees back 8 to 15 times, then follow with 8 to 15 fast repetitions. Finish by rolling your seat bones back, arching your back slightly, and pulsing with your buns at knee level 30 times.

Injury Prevention
- Keep your eyes straight ahead.
- Keep your back flat and your chest up.
- Don't place your feet wider than your knees.

TAP, TAP, KICK

Works the gluteus maximus and minimus. After all, every bride benefits from a firmer derriere.

🔔   Position 1. Lie on your left side with your left hand supporting your head and your right forearm on the floor in front of you. Bend your knees, placing your thighs at a right angle to your torso.

🔔   Position 2. Lift your right heel and tap your right knee to your left knee. Now, lift the right knee and tap it to the left foot. Finally, extend your right leg straight out in front of your right hip. Hold and then repeat the sequence 8 to 15 times per side.

Injury Prevention

- Keep your body weight forward so that your top hip is directly over your bottom hip.

SIDE LEG LIFT

Works the gluteus maximus and outer thigh, and will help your legs feel long and lean.

⌂ Position 1. Lie on your left side with your left hand supporting your head and your right forearm on the floor in front of you. Stay relaxed in your upper body. Bend your left knee. Tip your pelvis under and extend your right leg straight and behind your hip 15 degrees.

⌂ Position 2. Flex your foot and move your leg 1 inch up and 1 inch down. Repeat 25 times on each side.

⌂⌂ After completing the initial repetitions, alternate flexing and pointing the toe while lifting for an additional 25 repetitions per side.

⌂⌂⌂ Bring your heel to your seat and kick it back out. Push from your seat all the way through your heel. Try 25 to 30 kicks out.

Injury Prevention

- Keep your pelvis tipped under.
- Don't arch your back.

BUN BURNER

Works your gluteus maximus and minimus. This one prepares you for any and everything!

🔔 Position 1. Lie on your back with your feet against a wall and your knees bent at 90 degrees. Press your knees, inner thighs, and feet together. Keep your upper body relaxed with your arms by your sides and maintain a "C" shape through your midsection.

🔔 Position 2. Slowly lift your bottom a few inches off the floor, contracting your gluteus. Imagine you have a quarter between your buns. Hold the contraction, squeeze, then lower your bottom back down within an inch of the floor. Pulse up and down 30 to 50 times.

🔔🔔 After the initial repetitions, turn your heels outward as though you were pigeon-toed. Press your knees together, squeeze your inner thighs, and pulse up and down 30 to 50 times.

🔔🔔🔔 Raise your right leg straight up and continue pulsing 30 to 50 times. Switch sides and repeat.

Injury Prevention

- Don't lift your lower back very high off the floor.
- Keep your upper body relaxed.
- Don't furrow your brow or grit your teeth. It won't make your bottom squeeze any tighter.

7

The Stress-Free Bride

On the list of anxiety and stress provokers, wedding preparation is surely close to the top. Not only are there so many things to plan, but also—inevitably—there is usually drama. Show me a bride-to-be whose planning is drama free and I'll buy her a cookie. Drama can come in all shapes and sizes. There's dress drama, bitchy bridesmaid drama, and bridal shower drama. Maybe you want a DJ and your fiancé wants a band, or he wants a small wedding and you want a big one. Sometimes there are divorced parents to deal with or embarrassing relatives who might put a damper on the festivities. The list goes on and on. People who have been otherwise normal in your life up to this point may begin to show some not-so-pleasant personality traits. You become the glue that holds it all together, and if you get stressed out, the potential for everything to fall apart becomes very real. And this time should be fun!

So, in an effort to help you stay fabulously composed and avoid adding therapy to your bridal registry, we've compiled some helpful tips for staying stress free during this hectic time.

CREATING SUPPORT SYSTEMS

Let's start with the obvious support system: your fiancé. Grooms are often looking to get in shape for the big day. They feel the same spotlight that is shining on you. The great thing about getting your fiancé involved is that you get to spend some quality time together while accomplishing your fitness goals. This will also encourage him to better understand your process and how to be there for you. All of the same rules of the Wedding Workout apply to him, only he can adjust the program to his own fitness level. You may get a real kick out of watching him try to conquer the flexibility section. By the way, how is his posture? He's going to be standing just as long as you are at the wedding. Get him involved!

Why not add your maid of honor to your Wedding Workout support team? I'm sure she or he (welcome to the modern wedding party) wants to look fab for the big day, too, especially if your maid of honor is single. You never know who you might meet or marry, and weddings are always a fun place to meet new people. While you're at it, you might solicit the whole bridal party to get involved in your workouts. You're probably going to be venting to your bridal party about all your wedding drama, so why not do it while you're exercising? I'm sure they'd be happy to listen to your fitness fiascos and triumphs, too. Group exercise can be really

Suzanne

Maybe your fiancé is like mine—six-foot-three with the metabolism of a professional athlete. He can sit down and eat a pound of pasta and lose weight. Ah, the irony of my life. He likes to exercise, but he isn't really interested in my modes of exercise. However, he is an amazing support system. He may not be out pounding the pavement with me during my cardio sessions, but he is pushing me out the door to get them done because he knows how important they are to me. I love my bed and sometimes it is really hard to get out of it to do my workout, but with his help I can do it. He is always supporting my efforts. He makes a conscious effort to remind me how great I'm doing or tell me how much he notices the changes in my body. If your fiancé is taking notice of the changes in your body, take the compliment to heart. He isn't trying to tell you that he didn't think you looked great before; he's just letting you know that you look even better now. This kind of encouragement is what will inspire you to stay on the program. So, the bottom line is if you can't get your fiancé to be your Wedding Workout buddy, get him to be one of your Wedding Workout coaches. After all, he is your biggest fan and I'm sure he wants you to win for yourself and for the team.

fun. You might start a weekly soccer game or road race. A spinning class followed by a cup of coffee is a great way to catch up and connect about wedding activities. Don't forget about your parents and future in-laws. Suzanne's whole family has been in fitness mode since she announced her engagement. If your parents and in-laws live in the same city, it might be fun to get them together for walks on the weekend. That way, they will have a chance to get to know one another rather than meeting for the first time at the rehearsal dinner. Everyone benefits. If you're feeling awkward about telling people you're on a plan, don't. Shout it out! The more you broadcast your commitment to working out, the more others can offer support and encouragement.

PARTNER STRETCHING

Now that you've convinced your fiancé to get involved, have him help you stretch. It's fun and physical and can be great foreplay. We double dare you to try these stretches in your birthday suits. Try these for a fun and effective partner stretch.

SPINAL TWIST

Sit on the floor with both legs extended. Bend your right leg and lift the right foot over the left leg. Place the sole of your foot next to your knee. Sit tall and elongate your back. Let your hands hang loosely behind you. Your fiancé should be behind you on his knees, slightly to your left. Take a deep breath. He should then press his chest into your back while simultaneously pulling your knee toward you and your right shoulder back toward him. Exhale as he helps you create a twisting sensation in your spine.

FORWARD BEND

For the deepest forward bend, have your fiancé lay his body weight on your back. Gradually use each breath to go deeper and deeper into the stretch. Don't try to reach your deepest point right off the bat. You want to crawl your forehead down your shins as though you are going to touch the top of your feet with the top of your head.

WIDE LEG FORWARD BEND

Sit wide-legged while face-to-face with your fiancé. Make sure the bottoms of your feet and his feet are pressed together. Clasp hands. Take turns leaning back toward the floor while pulling your partner toward you.

BALL STRETCH

Get into your ball position, place your feet on your fiancé's chest, and have him press your knees into your chest. For a deeper stretch, have him simultaneously press your upper thighs and hips down into the floor.

BEHIND THE HEAD SHOULDER-AND-CHEST OPENER

Sit cross-legged on the floor. Lace your fingers and clasp them behind your head. Your fiancé should be on his knees behind you. Have him bring his arms over and in front of your arms and gently pull back your elbows.

STRAIGHT-LEG PRESS

Start in your ball position, extending one leg out on the floor in front of you while bringing your other knee into your chest. Have your fiancé face you while resting on his knees. He should gently place one knee on your extended leg. Straighten your bent knee and place your calf against his shoulder in front of you. He should gradually bend toward you as though he is coming in for a little sugar (smooch).

When in Doubt, Breathe!

We have to give credit to our friend Melissa for this one. While using the restroom one day at Melissa's house, Suzanne noticed something curious taped to the mirror: the word *breathe*. "I read it a few times and then took in a long, slow, deep breath. I let it out very slowly and marveled at how fantastic it felt. I realized in that moment that I never take the time to just BREATHE. When I came out of the restroom, I noticed that she also had the word taped to the fridge and to a light switch. I was so intrigued that I had to find out the reason for the reminders. She explained to me that when she gets stressed out, she tends to hold her breath, which creates tension in her body. I started to ask my other friends and found that many of them had the same problem. I, myself, was never conscious of holding my breath during moments of stress or anxiety. However, during my wedding preparation, I have found that I have been more anxious than normal, so I've started to use the Melissa Method." So, brides-to-be, remember to BREATHE when times get crazy. If it helps, tape the word everywhere you can—in your car, on your computer, or on your mother's forehead! Who knows? If you take a deep breath when she's nagging you about the centerpieces, you might just make it through that moment without a fight.

Journaling

Writing can be incredibly therapeutic. We can vouch for that since writing this book! Sometimes putting thoughts on paper can bring clarity to perplexing or frustrating situations during wedding planning. Journaling is also nice because later you'll be able to look back through your writing to see how you were feeling during this time, and hopefully smile. Perhaps the journal pages we've created will offer some suggestions on what you want to include in your own journal. You may just want to keep a journal for lists and ideas that you have relating to your dream wedding. By putting pen to paper, you may be able to transfer your stress to the page, release it, and move on to more positive planning endeavors.

Massage

Ah, massage! If you've had one, you understand; and if you haven't, indulge yourself and you, too, will be saying, "Ah, massage." Too bad we don't live in the Far East where an hour massage costs just ten dollars. I'd probably have one every day. Eastern cultures have been hip to massage for centuries, praising its healing and therapeutic powers. We wacky westerners are always the last to catch on. Reflexology, massage that concentrates on pressure points in the feet, takes less time and usually costs less and you come out feeling like you've had a whole body massage. If you can't stretch your budget any further, ask your fiancé to play masseur. Why not order in food, light some candles, and let his fingers do the walking?

Making Love

Double aaah! Intimacy and love are the reasons you're getting married, after all. Let's not let your wedding preparations keep you from having intimate moments. Use them to your advantage. A little roll in the hay with your man may not exactly cover one of your cardiorespiratory sessions, but it certainly can be an exercise elective. You'll most certainly reduce your stress level and you'll burn some bonus calories to boot. Top it off with some hugs and kisses and you have a winning combination to help you tackle any planning paradox. And remember to breathe!

Beauty Retreat

A day at the salon will make most brides forget the perils of planning. A new hairdo might bring on a renewed attitude. Throw in a manicure and a pedicure and watch out, world! Go have a Brazilian bikini wax. It is a welcome enhancement whether you're in your bikini or your bridal buff. It also might be fun and a good stress reliever to go have your makeup done. You can explore makeup styles for your wedding day. Many of the makeup counters at the department stores will do your makeup for free or with a minimal purchase. You can get a jump start on your wedding look by working with one of the makeup artists to find out what colors will work best for you on the big day.

Bubble Baths

Grab some bubbles and aromatherapy oils and jump in. A bath is a cost-effective stress reliever and it sure feels good. Turn on some really good music, light a candle, and you have your own homemade spa.

Shopping

When all else fails, go shopping. If stress is what ails you, a trip to the mall is a surefire cure. You may have showers and parties that you need to shop for and leaving it to the last minute will just create more stress, so you have a good excuse to shop 'til you drop. We know budgets are tight during this time, but even a good window-shopping spree can ease tensions.

Closet Cleaning

Cleaning closets isn't just for spring anymore. As you prepare for your new life to unfold, a good closet cleaning can help you get rid of physical and emotional cobwebs of the past. Why not get rid of the old and make space for the new? You know, all the new clothes you'll be buying during your stress-free shopping spree. Invite a friend over to help you let go of those acid-washed jeans from high school. Take a bag of the old stuff and donate it to a women's center or to the Salvation Army. This will take your mind off of wedding planning and undoubtedly give you a sense of renewal.

Support Systems

Earlier in this chapter, we discussed creating support systems in relation to exercise. Support systems can also be beneficial during your wedding planning. My suggestion would be to pick a few friends whom you trust to bounce ideas off of or vent frustrations to. Your stress support system should be made up of people who can remain impartial. Therefore, I would advise against choosing someone too close to the situation, such as your mother or fiancé. They have their own stress levels to keep in check. Sometimes, it's just nice to call on a married girl-friend who's gone through the process to get her advice about wedding etiquette or to vent to about the flaky florist.

Laugh Off the Little Things

There are going to be frustrations. It's a fact of planning anything—especially a wedding. Your wedding day is supposed to be what you've always dreamt about, but often it turns into what everyone else wants it to be. The key is to keep a positive attitude and focus on the things you're doing right. Try to laugh about the little irritations and annoyances. We guarantee that looking at things with a sense of humor will ease the stress of things not going perfectly. You'll be able to enjoy yourself even more on the big day and smile all the way down the aisle.

Bridal Breakdown-Prevention Pointers

- Remember, it's YOUR WEDDING!
- Remember that your fiancé loves you.
- Focus on the positive.
- Bridal blunders are a sure thing. Try to manage them and don't let them stress you out.
- Let others who love you, help you.
- When all else fails, don't forget to laugh!

8

The Nutrition-Savvy Bride

Throughout *The Wedding Workout*, we've tried to stress the idea of balance in everything you do. Balancing time with your fiancé with time alone. Balancing your job with planning your wedding. Balancing intense training with moderate training. And most importantly, balancing your food intake with your energy expenditure. We've introduced you to three of the four components that make the Wedding Workout effective. Now we move to the all-important fourth component—clean eating.

CLEAN EATING VERSUS DIET DEPRIVATION

By clean eating we mean making conscious, informed, and positive food choices. The food choices you make have a direct influence on your success with the Wedding Workout. Try to think of your body as a Ferrari. To keep it running at peak performance, you need to fill it with high-octane, clean-running fuel. Regular unleaded will not do. We like the phrase *clean eating* because it represents foods that are fuel efficient for your body. We love food. It's one of the greatest things about life. Food should be enjoyed, but it is also the fuel that makes your body run smoothly. If you are eating "clean" foods in the right proportions, your body will act like an incinerator, utilizing the food you eat to produce the energy that you need, while achieving a healthy weight. That means that the food you're eating won't end up on your thighs but will actually be used for its real purpose, energy, and not stored as fat.

Perhaps you were raised with the notion that meat and potatoes are the fuel of champions. We're here to tell you that while meat and potatoes make for a tasty dinner, there are far better choices that you can make when deciding what to put into your body.

It's no coincidence that *diet* is a four-letter word. We'd almost rather utter another kind of four-letter word than have the word *diet* in our vernacular. Not to mention the first three letters of the word are D-I-E. The dictionary definition of the word *diet* is "the usual food and drink of a person or animal." But, if you look up the word in a thesaurus you might find synonyms such as "fast" or "starve oneself." Isn't that sad? People are always on a never-ending search for the next weight-loss answer. One problem with dieting (oops! we said it) is that people are so focused on looking good, they forget they should be focusing on feeling healthier. Another problem is that a change in eating habits has to be permanent in

Suzanne

As the bride-to-be, I've always had to watch my weight. Because I love food, I envy women who can eat whatever they want when they want it. I can gain weight simply by eating poorly over a single weekend. Sometimes after indulging in a brownie or a piece of cake, I can almost feel it planting itself on my rear end like a spaceship landing on the moon. Diet plan after diet plan, counting calories and counting carbs with no long-term success had left me feeling despondent about the joys of eating. Now, with Tracy's help, I've finally found a way to enjoy food again and enjoy the benefits of a fitness program. The combination of exercise and a healthy diet is what is working for me. I used to diet without really implementing a solid exercise program. I lost a few pounds, but my body really didn't change. The Wedding Workout has really changed my body and the nutrition program has now become a way of life. ℯ

order to maintain a weight loss and diets are so rigid that they are usually only a temporary solution. We don't want to be your codependent partners in the vicious cycle of crash dieting. We know it's just like being in a bad relationship. You experience the euphoria of the newness (pounds lost), which is then followed by the breakup or the binge. Then you find yourself back at it again, trying to achieve a different result. But clean eating can get you off the diet roller coaster and provide a way for you to reach a healthy weight while enjoying food.

We want you to focus on learning more about nutrition, and that includes everything you eat and drink. We want to increase your awareness and consciousness about eating well, despite your crazy schedule. Our recommendation isn't drastic, nor is it revolutionary. It's a simple suggestion for developing a healthier way of eating now and ever after.

We've both had our own experiences on the diet (oops! we said it again) hamster wheel. Have you ever seen a skinny hamster? They are always on that wheel and getting nowhere. Between the two of us we've done the Scarsdale Diet, the Atkins Diet, Weight Watchers, Jenny Craig, The Zone, and the Cabbage Soup Diet. Each time we thought we had found the new miracle weight-loss messiah. While all of these diets are effective in their own way, the overall programs were hard to maintain, thus explaining our very long list. We learned something from each program about what worked and what did not, thus helping us to create what we feel is a realistic approach to healthy eating.

Tracy

As a trainer, every day I have women asking me, "How can I lose weight? What should I be eating?" What I've learned is that people are confused about what to eat and aren't aware of the right amounts of food to eat. They know what healthy foods are, but they don't know how to execute healthy eating. Basically, I don't believe in cutting anything out and saying you can't have it. I believe in adopting the healthy habit of moderation and making healthy food choices. Banning foods that you really love just sets you up for failure and obsession. What you resist always persists. People come up to me all the time and tell me that they aren't eating pasta, bread, wheat, white flour, sugar, and fruit. I think to myself, what is there left to eat? Let's be realistic. I want you to make adjustments to your eating that will benefit you now and forever. You know your own body and what you crave. Work with those cravings and make them fit into your life. I think of it as self-parenting with your eating habits. You must avoid being too strict with children because most likely they will rebel down the line. On the other hand, you can't give children zero limitations because they go wild without structure and discipline. For me, self-parenting with food is a form of self-love. I'm consciously taking care of myself rather than neglecting my health.

No wonder eating has become a stress in women's lives rather than the joy it should be. For example, one of my clients came to me after class and explained that she was just eating protein and that she was doing cardio every day. I asked her how she felt and as the tears welled up in her eyes she answered, "MISERABLE!" I asked her if we could throw out her plan for a few days and then start a more balanced program. She was relieved! I explained to her what I call the "All or Nothing Mentality." By "all or nothing" I mean going to the extremes in all that you do: exercise, eating, cardio, and your thinking. In other words, in your mind you're either eating perfectly or poorly. The result is that you're either on one side of the pendulum, feeling in control and good about yourself, or on the other, feeling out of control and worthless. This type of "all or nothing" thinking is simply a setup for failure because it doesn't embrace living a balanced life. If you eat well all week and indulge on the weekend, the idea is not to let the pendulum swing into the negative but rather know that tomorrow is another day. What you've achieved will not be lost in a single weekend if you get back on track and resume clean eating. Remember, no one can maintain the "All" part of the "All or Nothing Mentality" all the time. Don't set yourself up to fail by going to extremes. Balance and moderation are the keys to true success. ☞

THE SKINNY ON SKINNY

If you look up the word *skinny* in a thesaurus it will have words such as *emaciated, haggard, starved,* and *gaunt.* We don't know about you, but we consider these words to be negative and contradictory to the idea of a healthy, positive woman who feels confident about herself. Still, many women we know want to catch what we refer to as the "skinny disease." It seems to be the one disease women want to have. Like a puppy on a leash with a collar that is too tight, we see women pushing, pulling, and hurting themselves while taking all the freedom and joy out of their lives just to get skinny. Strive to be healthy and happy. You want your fiancé to know he has a real woman who is comfortable in her own body. It's vitally important to like yourself, and conscious, clean eating can help you do that.

Tracy

During the few times when I have gotten too thin (i.e., after a breakup), I seem to get a lot more attention from women than from men. Women have become accustomed to believing in the skinny disease and adopting the mantra, "The thinner I am, the better." In fact, I often see one woman telling another woman she is too thin while at the same time trying to calculate how her friend got that way. While there are always exceptions to the rule, most of the men I know like to see a little meat on their woman's bones. I just ask that you don't buy into all the images presented to you on TV and in magazines and avoid the skinny disease. No bride looks beautiful when she is emaciated, gaunt, or starved.

CLEAN-EATING FUNDAMENTALS

Carb-Lite PM: Here's what we've found that really works for us, as well as for Tracy's clients, for the long haul. We call it Carb-Lite PM. After 4 PM, Sunday through Friday, we give starchy carbs (such as pasta, bread, potatoes, sugars, etc.) the boot until morning. The table below gives examples of starchy carbs, both whole grain and processed white flour, which we stay away from at night. We choose to eat these types of carbohydrates in the right proportions at breakfast or lunch.

STARCHY CARBOHYDRATES

BREADS	GRAINS	CEREALS	VEGETABLES
Bagel	Pasta	Oatmeal	Potatoes
Pancakes	Rice	Granola	Corn
Wheat roll	Couscous	Raisin bran	Peas

To us this feels like a great compromise between programs like The Zone and Atkins. These programs, albeit popular right now, seem too extreme for many people. Carb-Lite PM is attainable for more people. We really can do it and see results. We believe in having a balanced diet. There was just no way that we were going to give up bread for the rest of our lives and neither of us want to be made to feel unhealthy or destined for the fat farm if we eat it. We, like many others, love bread and we both consider eating one of the great joys in life. We all know that too much of one thing, however, whether it's protein or carbs, is not a good thing. The bottom line is that whether you gain or lose weight really depends on the balance of your total intake of calories versus the amount of calories you burn daily. The problem with carbohydrates is not that people are eating them; we are just eating too much of them. By following Carb-Lite PM, you will eat carbs for breakfast, lunch, and snacks before 4 PM, but you will simply avoid starchy carbs at dinner. I guarantee that you will wake up in the morning feeling less hungry and more energized.

Did you know that protein takes longer to be metabolized by your body than carbohydrates? When you eat starchy carbs at night, they get processed while you sleep, but because you are inactive excess calories from carbohydrates are turned to sugar and stored as fat rather than being utilized as fuel. Protein, because it takes longer to be metabolized and usually contains some fat, keeps you full through the night. When you wake up you can begin adding simple carbohydrates to your meals before 4 PM. By eating carbs during the day, you fuel your body for your daily activities and burn carbs as you eat them. As we've already discussed throughout *The Wedding Workout*, it is important to take breaks along the way. Carb-Lite PM is no different. Once a week, give yourself a day off so you can enjoy your favorite carbs after 4 PM. Your day off is not a license to go crazy, but it will allow you to take time to enjoy the foods you love at a party or on a date with your fiancé.

Eat at Least Four to Five Times a Day

Your eating plan should include three main meals and one or two snacks. It is important that you eat every three to four hours to keep your metabolism going and regulate your blood sugar. Have you ever been really irritable only to realize that you haven't eaten in five hours? We've all been there. To avoid this, first learn to love breakfast. When you eat breakfast you stamp your metabolism's timecard and send it off to work for the day. Every time you eat you rev your metabolism, which helps to burn fat. That's why your snacks are so important. Eating a mid-morning snack and an afternoon snack helps to curb your appetite at lunch and dinner.

Drink Water

Drink at least 64 ounces of water a day or eight 8-ounce glasses. Make water your maid of honor. Take water with you wherever you go and you will reap the amazing benefits of her friendship. Water, among its many attributes, aids in digestion and food absorption, and removing toxins and other wastes from our bodies. Two-thirds of our body weight is made up of water, so our bodies literally can't live without it. Water not only has zero calories but also serves as an appetite suppressant and flushes out the by-products of fat metabolism. Drinking water is great for your skin, too. Here's another interesting fact about water: If you don't drink enough of it, your body will retain it to make up for the shortage and you will feel bloated. The key is to drink more water, not less. Drink eight glasses a day and enjoy every ounce of nature's miracle.

FOOD FIT FOR A BRIDE: WHAT TO EAT AND HOW MUCH

We've told you *how* you should eat on the Wedding Workout; now we are going to tell you what to eat and how much. A balanced diet comprises protein, carbohydrates, and fat.

Protein comes in all shapes and sizes, animal and vegetable, and includes such stars as meat, poultry, fish, eggs, cheese, and soy products. Because you will be very active while on the Wedding Workout, your body's protein needs will increase. Try to add a form of protein at every meal. Protein is essential for building muscle mass and is needed for musculoskeletal training.

Carbohydrates come in two types: complex and simple. Complex carbohydrates primarily include vegetables, whole grains such as oatmeal, and starches made from white flour, such as pasta and bread. Simple carbohydrates include sugars. On Carb-Lite PM, we want you to stay away from starchy, complex carbs and simple sugary ones at night. But you can consider vegetables your nighttime friend. Carbohydrates are essential for fueling your muscles and brain. They are the first nutrient to be used by your body for energy.

Fats also come in two types: saturated and unsaturated. Saturated fats are found in animal products, such as butter and meat. Unsaturated fats are vegetable based and are found in oils, such as olive and canola, as well as in fruits and nuts such as avocados, olives, and almonds. We suggest that you shy away from saturated fats, which are known to contribute to heart disease. Unsaturated fats are healthy fats and add important nutrients to keep us looking and feeling good. Without them, our bodies have difficulty absorbing some essential vitamins from the foods we eat. Additionally, a little fat in your healthy eating plan will keep you feeling satisfied from meal to meal.

Your meals don't have be a perfect combination of protein, fat, and carbs every time, but your overall daily intake should reflect a balance of the right kinds and amounts of nutrients. One of the nutrients we encourage you to include in your diet is fiber. Fiber can be found in breads, grains, cereal, fruits, and vegetables. There are two kinds of fiber: soluble and insoluble. Soluble fiber, which is found in such things as oatmeal, barley, and beans, aids in the production and elimination of cholesterol by the body. Insoluble fiber, which is found in vegetables, fruits, wheat bran, and cereals, helps keep us regular. The key is determining how much fiber is enough. The recommended daily dose is between 25 to 35 grams a day. Try to eat a variety of fiber-rich foods throughout the day so you can benefit from both types. If you are new to fiber, start incorporating it into your diet slowly, as it can cause gas and bloating. Add more beans and vegetables to your diet and not only will you increase your fiber intake, but you will also be eating great sources of protein and carbohydrates in one shot.

For the Wedding Workout daily meal plan, we suggest that our brides-to-be focus on carbohydrate-rich breakfasts, such as oatmeal or fiber-rich cereal. Lunch should include lean protein with an abundance of vegetables. You can also have a small serving of starchy carbohydrates, such as a slice of rye toast or a handful of pretzels. Snacks can consist of a slice of an apple and a handful of almonds or lowfat cheese and a few slices of turkey. Your dinner plate should be filled with chicken, fish, lean meats, tofu, and vegetables of all sorts with an emphasis on leafy greens.

If you are a vegetarian, there are a lot of options for you. There are great soy products available, such as tofu and soybeans. We love veggie burgers, and protein powder is a great thing to add to oatmeal or smoothies to help you get that added protein. For maximum results, we encourage you to limit your alcohol and caffeine intake during the week. Both alcohol and caffeine are diuretics and cause water loss in the body due to increased urination. Not only do alcohol and caffeine dehydrate you, but they also drain you of essential minerals such as magnesium, potassium, and zinc. Additionally, by and large alcohol is next to sugar in the empty calorie department. Also, the dehydration associated with drinking alcohol can bring on the munchies. We appreciate the benefits of alcoholic beverages in moderation, such as red wine, which has been associated with reducing cholesterol.

Fruity, tropical mixed drinks and tonic cocktails, on the other hand, can be a nemesis to any workout and weight-loss goals. In addition to packing on extra calories, you will risk decreasing your workout performance. We want you to eliminate drinking during the week. If that seems unrealistic to you, limit yourself to one or two drinks a week and have that martini on your off day. For a lower calorie choice, try switching to lite beer or wine spritzers. If you have a taste for wine, you may also crave sweets. We haven't forgotten about your sweet tooth because we have them, too. We'll give you some tips later on about how to satisfy those cravings.

Here's how your daily servings should break down:

Protein: 3 servings, or 10 ounces
Dairy: 2–3 servings, or 1,000 mg of calcium (if you are sensitive to dairy)
Vegetables: 5–6 servings
Fruit: 2–3 servings
Breads/Starches: 6 servings
Fats: 3–4 servings

We also recommend that you take a daily multivitamin with iron. Also, be sure to get additional calcium in a supplement whether you're eating dairy or not. Finally, we don't encourage a bedtime snack because if you eat extra calories at night you won't have the chance to really use them until the morning. We guarantee that you'll wake up feeling great! If you find, however, that you're starving before you hit the sack, try one of our favorites: an apple and some peppermint tea.

The table on page 193 provides a sample menu for a day on the Wedding Workout Clean-Eating Plan.

SAMPLE MENU FOR THE WEDDING WORKOUT CLEAN-EATING PLAN

BREAKFAST	SNACK	LUNCH	SNACK	DINNER
1 slice multigrain toast with 1 tsp. peanut butter and ½ cup of lowfat cottage cheese OR 1 cup oatmeal with dried raisins or apricots OR **Suzanne's Super Smoothie***	1 string cheese and an apple OR ½ cup of nonfat yogurt, a small amount of nuts, and 1 graham cracker	Turkey or veggie burger on whole wheat bread with mustard OR **Wedding Workout Glazed Tofu Sandwich*** OR Salad with grilled chicken, light dressing, and a wheat roll	1 low-carb energy bar OR Celery with goat cheese	Fish with steamed vegetables and a salad with light dressing OR Grilled chicken with sautéed spinach and steamed broccoli OR **Tracy's Chicken Primavera***

*RECIPES AT END OF CHAPTER

The Hand Method

How do you figure out how much is too much? We've got a great method that travels well. We know that you've got a lot on your plate (ha, ha!), so we want to make portion sizing flexible and fun for you. The idea of measuring food on a scale or with measuring cups may feel too constraining, especially if you are always on the go. The easiest way to assess portion size, especially when dining out, is the Hand Method. We suggest using your left hand because you'll see your engagement ring, which will undoubtedly motivate you. However, you can't use your engagement ring in the equation, especially if it's a four-carat diamond. That could add up to a lot of extra calories. Here's how it works.

> Your open palm in shape and thickness = a 3–4 oz. serving of meat, fish, or poultry
>
> Your closed fist = 1 serving of starchy carbohydrates (pasta, rice, roll, etc.) or 1 fruit serving
>
> Your thumb = 1 fat serving (salad dressing, olive oil, etc.)
>
> Your four fingers outstretched flat = a 1 oz. serving of cheese
>
> Your palm open and cupped = 1 serving of vegetables

We think this is the best method for the busy bride. We do suggest, however, that if you have no idea what a cup of pasta or a teaspoon of olive oil looks like, you pull out your kitchen measuring tools in the beginning to get an idea. If you love using measuring cups and scales when cooking at home, be our guest. The Hand Method may not be as accurate as a measuring cup, but we find it the most realistic for use in everyday life and for success on the Wedding Workout.

The Nutrition Registry

We've given you the tools to eat healthfully, but we have another tool that will help you succeed: the nutrition registry. Think of the nutrition registry like your wedding registry; some things you've got, but some things you need. How do you figure out what's coming and going? It's all written down and recorded. Maybe you've gotten two place settings of your china but still need six more. The nutrition registry serves the same purpose for your eating plan. By keeping this food diary, you will be able to see how many servings of protein or carbs you've eaten for the day and where you need to balance out your choices. (See page 221 in the appendix.)

Your nutrition registry will reveal a lot about you. By writing down what you eat, you will be able to identify the areas that need to change. Maybe you need more protein in your diet or you're not eating enough fruits and vegetables. The other important thing about using the nutrition registry is that it helps you stay focused, honest, and conscious of what you're eating. Also, if you haven't made great food choices, you can look back at choices that brought greater success and use that information to motivate you to get back on track. Not to mention, what you eat has a significant impact on your workouts. So, if you're feeling sluggish, you might be able to target the problem and see patterns in your energy levels and exercise performance by reviewing what you've eaten.

Before beginning the Wedding Workout clean-eating program, it is important to understand your current relationship with food. It is only by understanding the role food plays in your life that you will be able to make a real change in your health and in your lifestyle. How do you relate to food? Start out by recording everything you eat and drink for three days, uncensored, in your nutrition registry before starting on the program. We don't want you to change what you eat; we just want you to keep an accurate account of what you normally eat. Add on information such as the time you eat and how you are feeling at that time. Are you slightly hungry or ready to chew off your left hand? All these feelings are factors in redefining your relationship with food. We simply want to take a realistic inventory of how you are eating now so you will know what you must work on. Awareness is always the first step leading to change. You would be surprised how many people thought they were eating well only to learn that they were coming up short in many food groups and slipping in a lot of empty calories.

After three days, take colored pens or highlighters and use one color per food group to circle the number of proteins, carbohydrates, fats, and glasses of water you consumed during the three days. Compare the results to the proposed daily servings we have allotted you in the clean-eating program. Based on our suggestions, you would ideally consume 9 protein, 9 dairy, 12 vegetable, 6 to 9 fruit, 18 bread, and 9 to 12 fat servings over the course of three days. Additionally, you would have consumed at least 24 glasses of water.

The Three Es

You might be in a hurry to start the program, but there is a method to this madness. I call it examine–educate–execute. By writing down everything you eat, you will be able to examine your relationship with food. With that information, you will then be able to educate yourself about making better choices when eating. Ask yourself why you eat certain foods at certain times. Raise your awareness about what you're putting into your body and why. Finally, when you execute you will be putting the clean-eating plan into action by replacing compulsive eating experiences with positive and rewarding ones. You will have the power over food!

Your Bridal Grocery Bag

Are you familiar with healthy restaurants near your home or work? Have you learned about healthy snack options and food options so you can be ready and prepared instead of giving in and racing to the nearest drive thru? Finally, have you stocked your refrigerator with yummy, healthy food choices?

We women, and especially brides-to-be, like shopping sprees of any kind. So, now that you're armed with the tools, head to the market. The table on page 197 provides a basic guideline of what kinds of things you should add to your pantry so that making positive food choices will be a breeze. We like to think of it as "strategic shopping."

BASIC PANTRY GUIDELINE LIST

PROTEIN	CARBOHYDRATES	FATS	FRUITS AND VEGETABLES	FREE FOODS
Skinless chicken breasts	Oats	Olive oil (try an olive oil spritzer to minimize amounts used)	Bagged lettuce	Herbs and spices
Lean luncheon meats	Fiber-enriched cereal (look for cereals with 5g at least—i.e., Total, Shredded Wheat, and Kashi)		Spinach	Mustard
Soy products		Canola oil	Broccoli	Salsa
Fish	Brown rice	Nuts	Tomatoes	Flavored vinegars
Cheese (lowfat; string)	Whole grain breads	Peanut butter	Carrots	
Yogurt	Wheat pasta	Avocados	Zucchini	
Skim or 1% milk	Beans (canned beans are great when time is a factor)	Olives	Mushrooms	
Lowfat cottage cheese		Reduced-fat salad dressings	Dark green leafy greens (romaine, baby, arugula, watercress)	
Eggs and/or Egg Beaters			Berries (frozen, great for smoothies)	
			Apples	
			Oranges	
			Melons	
			Banana (in moderation; high in sugar)	
			Pineapple (in moderation; high in sugar)	

Tracy

I usually go to the store following a run or my Sunday night class. I make a point of not shopping when I am ravenous. I deliberately take my time going down each aisle, sussing out all the goodies. I decide what I want to eat for the following week based on the "clean eating" principles. I load up on all the good, healthy stuff I can find so that I never feel deprived. In fact, when I unload all the bags and put the food away I get a healthy, nourished, and complete feeling because I really know that I'm taking care of myself. I feel excited and inspired when I open the refrigerator door and it is packed with great things to eat. A full fridge is a sure sign that I'm on the right track, as opposed to an empty one that leaves me feeling lonely, deprived, and like I must be on some awful diet. For some reason, whenever I need to focus on my health and fitness, the trip to the grocery store really helps me set the ball in motion. I feel stocked, prepared, and ready to go!

Suzanne

Getting married, trying to stay healthy, and going to the market can be a dizzying experience. Add to that cohabitating with a human trash compactor. I go to the market with a list and a week's meal plan in hand. I need to decide on meals that I can eat on the Wedding Workout and ones that will satisfy my fiancé. Generally, we can eat the same things. I just opt for smaller portions and at night I stay away from starches. I feed them all to him. Naturally, if both you and your fiancé are trying to get in shape for your wedding, he will be only too happy to join you in Carb-Lite PM. My fiancé likes a good cookie and a pint of ice cream. Because I don't want him to feel deprived, I still buy him his favorite treats, but I make sure they are not temptation foods for me. For example, he loves Ben & Jerry's Chunky Monkey, which is made with banana ice cream and chocolate chunks. Yuck! Banana ice cream wouldn't tempt me even if it was slathered all over my man's naked body. The point is that keeping his taste buds satisfied and your commitment to the Wedding Workout can go hand in hand. If you are a bride-to-be who is living alone, get to know the healthy restaurants in your neighborhood. If you don't like to cook just for yourself, try picking up a baked chicken from the market. You can use it for four different meals throughout the week. Shred it for salads or soft tacos. Toss it with scrambled eggs in the morning or eat it plain with steamed veggies. ⌐

BRIDAL CLEAN-EATING TRICKS

Here are some basic food tricks to help make clean eating easier and more fun.

1. Keep a glass of water by your bed and as soon as your morning alarm sounds, drink it down before you do anything else. It feels great and you'll get a jump start on meeting your daily water needs.

2. Buy individually packed snacks because a good-size portion is already determined for you.

3. Squeeze lemon or lime juice into your water to make for a refreshing treat.

4. Pack nonperishable, healthy snacks (almonds, sunflower seeds) in your glove compartment or your purse so that you don't just reach for anything when you get hungry.

5. For a helpful detox, squeeze lemon juice into an 8-ounce glass of hot water or try green tea, which contains antioxidants.

6. When dining out, figure out your portion size and have the rest of the food boxed up to go. Your doggy bag will make for a great lunch the next day.

7. Drink a glass of water before each meal. You will already feel full before you've even put fork to mouth.

8. Add more fiber to your diet. It will fill you up and keep you regular.

9. Keep written reminders around to drink water, eat slowly, or think before you eat. Don't watch TV or talk on the phone while you eat. You want to be fully present and experience your meals.

10. Count sixteen consecutive gulps before putting your water glass or bottle

down. Surprise! You've just chugged down about 8 ounces of water without even knowing it.

11. Find alternatives for your favorite fatty sweets. If chocolate seduces you, try to fall for a cup of lowfat hot chocolate or a nonfat latte instead. If strawberry pie is your thing, opt for strawberries and some nonfat whipped cream or a frozen sorbet bar or Popsicle.

12. Finally, remember that tomorrow is another day.

Creating Trust with Food

So many of us feel out of control when it comes to food. It is as though food is the big, crazy monster that sucks us in and we have no power to defend ourselves. Food, in and of itself, has no power. It's just food, and yet we assign all sorts of thoughts, feelings, and behaviors to it. We are afraid to take on healthy eating habits for fear of deprivation and boredom. These irrational fears cause us to continue with our poor eating habits. Let's look at it from another angle. Have you ever put money away to save up for something special? Each time you drop a quarter in the piggy bank, you're building up your nest egg. Simultaneously, dropping that quarter in creates a sense of confidence and security. You're building up a personal trust, which you will be able to depend on. Likewise, when you make positive food choices, you increase your trust with yourself in relation to food. Every healthy food choice you make is an empowering one. Every time you choose an apple over a cookie, you will learn that you have self-discipline and you are capable of making choices that make you feel good. You can do it! You will build up a reservoir of clean-eating confidence and you will be able to trust yourself with food.

Trigger Foods, Comfort Foods

Each of us has our own trigger foods. These are the foods that we don't want to live without because they satisfy very specific cravings. If you could only eat three foods for the rest of your life regardless of nutritional value, what would they be? Those foods represent your trigger foods. By trigger foods, we mean the foods that once you start eating, you can't stop. They're the ones that cause you to take a quick turn away from healthy choices into a downward spiral of sweets, starches, candy, and more candy. If you are unaware of which foods trigger you, start paying close attention. Trigger foods set off what we call "empty eating." By empty eating, we mean eating without being conscious. It's almost like sleepwalking. Sleepwalkers wake up wondering how they ended up naked in the lobby of their apartment building. Empty eating happens in a similar way. The hardest part about empty eating is that often we're unaware that we're doing it. The emotion that we feel takes over and drives the empty eating behavior. In this state, we can polish off a bag of chips or sour gummy bears in 0.5 seconds and barely remember what we've done. The problem is that the emotion remains and so do the calories.

No matter what your comfort or trigger foods may be, get clear on what they are and what they mean to you. Ask yourself, do I really need this to feel good? Then work really hard to replace compulsive empty eating with some other kind of positive, self-loving action. Taking a hot bath, treating yourself to a new lipstick, writing in your journal, or cuddling with your fiancé are great alternative responses to a food craving. Take an action that will fill you up. When you feel sad, depressed, or low, go against the feeling and make yourself get active. Don't throw

Tracy

Before straying from the program, ask yourself, "Why am I eating these cookies or chips?" Is there a certain feeling or comfort that you're looking for at the bottom of the bag? I've noticed how different foods elicit different feelings from me. For example, red licorice and gummy bears bring back positive childhood memories. When I want to feel grounded, I crave salty food such as pretzels and pickles. When I want to feel like someone is wrapping me up in a warm blanket, I want pizza. When I feel anxious, a nice bowl of cereal or yogurt helps to soothe my stomach. Finally, when I want to feel loved, there is no doubt I want chocolate. There is a time and place for all of these feelings and for all of these foods. No foods are bad. They just need to be balanced.

away all the hard work you've achieved by letting the negative, slothful feelings win out. You are too important!

Examine your relationship with food and you can learn a lot about who you are and what you need emotionally. Then go get what you need from your friends or by doing something nice for yourself. Be your own best parent, friend, and emotional support. Don't rely on food to do it for you. That's not its purpose. Food is nourishment for your body and soul. It keeps you alive so you can love others and yourself.

ENJOYING THE FESTIVITIES

The time between getting engaged and getting married is undoubtedly one of the most exciting and memorable times of any woman's life. There are parties, showers, and more parties and showers all in your honor. Inevitably, you will be the focus of all these events and that ol' spotlight will be shining on you. Oh, and we can't forget the visits to the caterer and cake maker to sample food for your wedding menu. Yum!

But there's a reason it is called sampling rather than gorging. The question is, how do you stay focused on eating well and still enjoy the festivities? Well, that's the beauty of the Wedding Workout program. Even though you will have to follow Carb-Lite PM six days a week, you get the reward of taking one day a week off. So, you can use that day for your shower, your bachelorette party, menu sampling, or date night with your man. It's up to you! If your coed shower is on a Friday night, then get right back on the plan Saturday morning. There's also a bonus for your body in taking a day off. You see, your body gets used to any routine after a while and you hit a plateau. By eating what you want within moderation one day a week, you jump-start your metabolism out of its familiar zone and you burn fat. If you have several events in one week, try to stick within the guidelines as much as possible. We're sure that if you ask nicely, the people that are throwing parties for you will work to provide healthy, tasty dishes that both you and your guests can enjoy. However, you also need to enforce positive choices that will make you feel good. Here's a list of tips that will make the festivities a breeze to handle and memorable as well.

FESTIVITY FOOD TIPS

1. Have a light snack before you head to the party so that you aren't ready to inhale the hors d'oeuvre tray.

2. Have a tall glass of sparkling water as soon as you get there; this will help curb your hunger and keep you hydrated.

3. Don't socialize near the buffet table. Mingle with your guests, not with the finger foods.

4. Don't eat just because other people are eating.

5. Go for high-protein food such as shrimp, turkey, or chicken. These choices will keep you satisfied longer.

6. Go for cheese if the only other choices are pigs in a blanket or buffalo wings.

7. Fill up on high-fiber foods such as carrots and celery.

8. Instead of crackers, which can be high in sugar, try a better choice such as French or rye bread if available.

9. Have a small taste of everything you want so that you don't feel deprived.

10. Hit the sweets last because you will have already eaten substantial foods and protein and won't binge on dessert.

11. If you must drink alcohol, alternate each drink with a glass of water. Not only will you stay hydrated, you won't become a babbling, boozing bride.

12. If Aunt Fannie has cooked up her famous praline caramel pie that she only makes once every five years, it is okay to splurge. Just make sure that you consciously choose to make an exception that you feel good about.

13. If you have a say in the menu, say it! It's okay to request special foods.

The Week Before

Whether you are wearing a form-fitting sheath or not, you still need to watch out for the three little devils: salt, alcohol, and caffeine. The closer you get to the big day, the more important it is to limit these items in your diet. Salt can make you bloated by causing you to retain water. Stay away from Asian cuisine, which includes a lot of soy sauce. Also, don't eat anything pickled or processed. Alcohol will dehydrate you, so try our tip about alternating a drink with a glass of water. Try to limit your intake of sodas, iced tea, coffee, and chocolate, all of which contain caffeine. Caffeine can cause jitters and we know that you don't need any more than the natural ones. Also, caffeine tends to bring you up and then send you crashing down, and you will need every ounce of energy you have.

Bridal Breakfast

On the big day you are going to need all your energy. We suggest that you eat a good breakfast that includes both protein and healthy carbohydrates so that you will be fueled all day and your blood sugar level will remain stable. We don't want you to have a bridal breakdown. Eating all your snacks today will be especially important in keeping you alert and energized, especially if you're having an evening wedding. Make sure you have eaten enough during the course of the day so that you aren't ravenous while you're exchanging vows. Plus, drinking on an empty stomach is not a good idea. If your nerves wake you up and make your stomach upset, try drinking some herbal tea or eating a couple of crackers. Don't forget that a run, walk, or set of push-ups will cut the anxiety. Slip a workout session into your wedding day and I guarantee that you'll feel amazing when you put your dress on. If your nervousness continues all day, it might be time to take that shot of vodka before you head down the aisle.

Here are a few meal ideas that will keep you going on your wedding day.

Fruit smoothie

1 egg with 1 slice of toast and peanut butter

½ bagel with light cream cheese or a slice of cheese

Cottage cheese and banana

Nonfat yogurt and strawberries

Oatmeal with dried fruit and nuts

Chicken or tuna salad

Cheese omelet

Try to stay away from raw vegetables, which may leave you feeling gassy or bloated—two things you don't want on your big day.

CONGRATULATIONS!

You made it! Your hard work and commitment to the Wedding Workout has paid off and you should congratulate yourself on achieving your fullest potential as an individual as you take your strongest self to be joined with your fiancé in marriage. It's your day. Indulge! If you want to eat your entire wedding cake on your own, go for it! Eat, drink, and be married.

RECIPES

Suzanne's Super Smoothie

- ½ cup nonfat plain yogurt
- 1 cup mixed frozen berries
- ½ cup orange juice
- 1 large tablespoon protein powder (optional)

Place all the ingredients in a blender and blend until smooth. Yum!

MAKES 1 SERVING.

Tracy's Chicken Primavera

- 1 teaspoon olive oil
- 2 cups steamed veggies (broccoli, carrots, cauliflower, etc.)
- 1 skinless, boneless chicken breast (cut into cubes)
- 1 ½ cups lowfat, ready-made pasta sauce (Classico, Newman's Own)

Heat olive oil in a large sauté pan. Add steamed veggies and sauté 1 to 2 minutes. Add cubed chicken and cook thoroughly for 5 to 6 minutes. Add pasta sauce and heat through for another 2 to 3 minutes. Salt and pepper to taste. Enjoy!

MAKES 1 SERVING.

Wedding Workout Tofu Sandwich

- 1   14-ounce package of firm tofu, drained and cut into 8 slices, $\frac{1}{2}$-inch thick
- 1   teaspoon olive oil
-     pinch of salt
-     pinch of black pepper
- $\frac{1}{4}$ cup Worcestershire sauce
- $\frac{1}{3}$ cup lowfat mayonnaise
- $\frac{1}{3}$ cup chopped fresh basil
- 1   garlic clove, minced
- 8   slices whole wheat bread, toasted
- 8   slices of tomato, $\frac{1}{4}$-inch thick

Dry the tofu. Heat olive oil in a large nonstick skillet over medium-high heat. Add tofu and sauté for 4 minutes. Turn tofu over, sprinkle with salt and pepper, and sauté for 4 more minutes. Spoon Worcestershire sauce over tofu and cook 30 seconds or until browned, turning once.

Combine mayonnaise, basil, and garlic. Spread mayonnaise mixture evenly over 4 slices of bread, then layer each with 2 tofu slices and 2 tomato slices. Cover with remaining bread slices.

MAKES 4 SERVINGS.

9

The Honeymoon and Ever After

Back in Babylonia some four thousand years ago, couples would get married under a full moon. The father of the bride would then get his new son-in-law and daughter trashed on mead or honey beer every night for thirty days. Thus, we have the humble beginnings of the honeymoon. There is also another myth about the evolution of the honeymoon. In ancient times, marriages often came about by capture instead of choice. Carl the caveman would whisk off his less than enthusiastic bride-to-be to a hiding place where they would drink honey beer for thirty days. By the time her family found her, the bride would already be with child. As far as we're concerned, the honeymoon was quickly over.

Wow, how times have changed! While our mothers and grandmothers didn't have to worry about being kidnapped, they did have to deal with wedding night jitters. While this is still a concern for some modern brides, the majority of us are busy worrying about whether our Wedding Workout bods look better in a string bikini or a one-piece. How about that matching sarong and platform flip-flops? Not to mention, we're fretting over how much SPF we need and which self-tanner won't turn us orange.

All things considered, we've got some pointers for you that are sure to make bathing-suit shopping easier. Here come those fabulous Diamond Girls, only now they're all married. Presenting Mrs. Pear-cut Girl. Not every bathing-suit style is going to flatter her unique shape, but before there's too much drama, we'll find her one that does. Bathing-suit shopping is not fun for anyone, even for thin women with zero hips. Just ask Mrs. Emerald. Do not believe what you see in the dressing-room mirror! What they don't tell you is that they buy those mirrors wholesale from the local funhouse. The lighting is straight out of a horror movie and shows every dimple, vein, wrinkle, mole, pimple, or bulge in graphic, grotesque detail. Bathing-suit shopping is right up there on the top of the stress list with moving, starting a new job, wedding planning, and shopping for jeans. We hope we can make your search a little easier.

First of all, grab your most honest yet loving friend. Plan for a fun day. Maybe you want to schedule lunch at your favorite café after the agony is over. Be sure to be very kind and comforting to yourself. Bathing-suit shopping induces negative self-talk like no other activity. Be prepared for those voices to arise and don't let them get the best of you.

If you're a Pear-cut girl, fuller on the bottom and in the hips, a darker-colored suit will help to give you a slimmer look. Look for breast-enhancing tops that will help draw attention away from your hips and thighs and balance out your over-all figure.

If you are small busted, go for padded tops with built-in bras. To further accentuate what you've got, look for tops with lighter-colored borders or piping. For large-busted brides, steer clear of padded bra tops. Your best bet are tops with underwire or halter styles that will visually give your shoulders a more narrow look. Also, any top with more fabric will provide you with more coverage.

If you are a Heart-cut girl, you might try balancing a halter top or high-neck racer-back top with a skort or skirt suit bottom, both of which will add full-ness to your lower half. If your tummy is the trouble, try a one-piece with a waist minimizer.

Brides with short torsos should try tube-top styles with lower-cut bottoms to create length through the midsection. Brides with long torsos should try tankini-style suites because the versatile, sporty tops can be worn long or short depending on how much of your midsection you want to reveal.

Tankini suits and suits with sport-short bottoms are great for athletic fig-ures or Princess-cut girls. They are fashioned after popular athletic wear styles, so if you are used to wearing these styles in the gym, go for it. They are also perfect for playing volleyball, football, water sports, or Frisbee on the beach—anytime you don't want to risk unintentional breast baring. But if you're into that, take your honeymoon in Europe; just spare your mother-in-law from seeing the pictures.

Finally, Diamond Girls should stay away from crazy patterns, heavy florals, and shiny metallic suits if they don't want to call attention to feature flaws. However, Emerald-cut girls might want to try these fabrics because they will add fullness to their lean figures. Above all, remember that basic black is always your most flattering friend.

HONEYMOON EATING

You know the deal: airport food and airplane food—the deadly duo. Most likely you will be traveling to some exotic land for your honeymoon, and you will have to arrive at the airport at least two hours before your flight. In my experience, waiting time at the airport can often lend itself to empty eating, and then some. In other words, fun food is entertainment and can help the time fly by. To prevent a fun food airport frenzy, I suggest eating a good meal before you arrive at the airport. If, however, you feel the need to eat right before you get on board, be encouraged by the fact that the American Dietetic Association examined food selections in airports across the country. Their findings suggest that airport food has greatly improved in nutritional value due to healthier food choices becoming more readily available within the terminals. You may have to look a little further, beyond McDonald's and other fast-food choices, but you can usually find salads, fresh fruit, turkey and tuna sandwiches, bagels, and lowfat yogurt. Following the coffeehouse trend, many airports now have specialty coffee shops. But be careful because this is where the muffins, high-fat pastries, and desserts are hiding out.

Once you get on the plane, the lack of anything better to do can once again increase your temptation to eat. Unless you have determined that your travel day will be your free day, remember your plan is to maintain your clean-eating habits. No sense wasting your free day on food that is less than spectacular or not what you really want anyway. As we all know, airplane food is generally a hand-grenade-size portion of an explosive combination of carbs and fats. Those cheesy, saucy processed meals with bread and rich desserts can't compare to having a gourmet meal at your favorite restaurant or honeymoon getaway. Think about where you would prefer to splurge and make the positive choice.

All too often we throw healthy eating right out the window as soon as we are away from home. It is because we are no longer in the comfort of our daily routine. The point of traveling is to be free, relax, and have fun, but you don't want to forget you were ever doing the Wedding Workout. Hopefully, your new habits will be such an integral part of your life by then that you will be excited to continue them in the first few days of newlywed bliss. Remember: Travel and the Wedding Workout can go hand in hand.

To take the Wedding Workout with you, get prepared before you travel. I suggest adding travel foods to your carry-on bag. Some items you might include are lowfat yogurt, dried fruit, almonds, apples, celery, and carrot sticks. You might even want to make a turkey sandwich for the trip. Just watch how the guy across the aisle salivates, wishing he had your sandwich instead of his dried-out chicken cordon bleu. Try calling ahead to the airline and requesting a special meal for both you and your husband. You can choose from low-calorie, vegetarian, diabetic, or kosher meals.

Most importantly, drink water! Include your water bottle in your carry-on and drink a glass at least every hour of the flight. Traveling by plane is always dehydrating because of the low humidity and recirculating air. Drinking lots of water will keep you hydrated and help prevent jet lag. You may have to use the lavatory a lot, but at least you get to stretch your legs and burn a few extra calories. If you get stuck in an airport, look at it as an opportunity to walk. You could even run up and down the terminal and people will just think you are late for your flight.

THE WEDDING WORKOUT FOR LIFE

The whole reason that you bought this book and began this program is because you had a specific target in sight: your wedding day. Our guess is that the typical honeymoon is about eight days. Hopefully, your honeymoon will be long enough for you to relax, enjoy yourself and your new body, and recover from your wedding. We hope it is everything you want it to be and more! Even after the chairs have been stacked, the tables have been put away, and the band has gone home, we're here to tell you that the honeymoon doesn't ever have to end. Don't let the post-wedding blues get the best of you. You will now need to focus on being the best wife you can be, which includes taking care of yourself.

Unfortunately, it is not uncommon for new brides to gain weight. It's not unlike gaining your freshman 15 in college. Everyone can warn you about it, but somehow it still creeps onto your thighs. We like to call it "the love butt." When you're in love and deliriously happy, it isn't hard to become complacent. As you settle into marital bliss, it is easy to enable each other to eat poorly and abandon working out. You want to grow old together, but that doesn't mean you have to grow old and fat together! The first year of marriage is often the most difficult year because of the many changes that you, as a couple, must face. This period of change can create a lot of stress. Stress can undermine even the best intentions to continue the program. Set new goals! Maybe one of your new goals is to maintain your weight or become more active by joining a coed team. Maybe you want to train for a marathon or a mini-triathlon. Or maybe you want to spend your first anniversary biking across France, so you'll need to stay in shape. Implement what you've learned and use your six-week cycles as stepping-stones to achieve your new goals and continue to be fit throughout your life. Don't allow yourself to lose what you have gained. You have the strength, power, and discipline to achieve whatever you want! You are in the driver's seat and you can maintain your fit Wedding Workout body for life. Each day, embrace your courage and willpower, and strive to express your own unique Diamond Girl style and energy to the world. Remember that you can make your life, and his, whatever you truly want it to be!

Appendix

WEEK OF:	CARDIO	ARMS	CHEST	PUSH-UPS	BACK	WAIST	ABDOMINALS	LOWER BODY
MONDAY	DURATION: TYPE: G M P ACTIVITY:	SETS ☐ ☐	SETS ☐ ☐	SETS ☐ ☐	SETS ☐ ☐	SETS ☐ ☐	SETS ☐ ☐	SETS ☐ ☐
TUESDAY	DURATION: TYPE: G M P ACTIVITY:	SETS ☐ ☐	SETS ☐ ☐	SETS ☐ ☐	SETS ☐ ☐	SETS ☐ ☐	SETS ☐ ☐	SETS ☐ ☐
WEDNESDAY	DURATION: TYPE: G M P ACTIVITY:	SETS ☐ ☐	SETS ☐ ☐	SETS ☐ ☐	SETS ☐ ☐	SETS ☐ ☐	SETS ☐ ☐	SETS ☐ ☐
THURSDAY	DURATION: TYPE: G M P ACTIVITY:	SETS ☐ ☐	SETS ☐ ☐	SETS ☐ ☐	SETS ☐ ☐	SETS ☐ ☐	SETS ☐ ☐	SETS ☐ ☐
FRIDAY	DURATION: TYPE: G M P ACTIVITY:	SETS ☐ ☐	SETS ☐ ☐	SETS ☐ ☐	SETS ☐ ☐	SETS ☐ ☐	SETS ☐ ☐	SETS ☐ ☐
SATURDAY	DURATION: TYPE: G M P ACTIVITY:	SETS ☐ ☐	SETS ☐ ☐	SETS ☐ ☐	SETS ☐ ☐	SETS ☐ ☐	SETS ☐ ☐	SETS ☐ ☐
SUNDAY	DURATION: TYPE: G M P ACTIVITY:	SETS ☐ ☐	SETS ☐ ☐	SETS ☐ ☐	SETS ☐ ☐	SETS ☐ ☐	SETS ☐ ☐	SETS ☐ ☐

EXERCISE REGISTRY

WEEK OF:	BREAKFAST	MORNING SNACK	LUNCH	AFTERNOON SNACK	DINNER	BEDTIME SNACK	NOTES
TIME							
MONDAY							
TUESDAY							
WEDNESDAY							
THURSDAY							
FRIDAY							
SATURDAY							
SUNDAY							

NUTRITION REGISTRY

Index